DEDICATION

This book is dedicated to teachers, instructors and school administrators, who are directly or indirectly involved in children education. Those who dedicate their time, striving to deliver quality education to children, regardless of the child's background, race and mental condition.

Also, Instructors who stood by the Montessori method of learning to exploit the latent ability in every child while still teaching morals and maintaining discipline.

ACKNOWLEDGEMENT

I will like to acknowledge the work and vision of Dr. Maria Montessori who laid down the path to educating children in a manner that will not only encourage them to learn ensure they learn without pressure.

While compiling this curriculum I have consulted the British children curriculum, Montessori primary guide (infomontessori.com) and the early years foundation curriculum, and Google image for graphic visuals that were edited and reformatted. With that I acknowledge the work of every major player that made this compilation a success. Also I will like to acknowledge the work of my Editor/Graphic designer and Co-writer, Ganiu Idris .A, your immense contribution is highly appreciated.

CONTENTS

INTRODUCTION

This is a learning guide written with details and clear illustrations process that will guide instructors/teachers towards delivering the best of Montessori education to children. This curriculum guide is meant to help young children get ready for school. It is a guide intended to lay the path to developing early literacy and learning skills for children.

Strong reading skills form the basis of learning in all subjects, it is, however, important to identify those who struggle with reading as early as possible.

This guide that was developed by the writer and thoroughly edited by the editor is currently in use by a Montessori school founded by the writer. We can testify that the book has made learning easy for children as much as it has also made teaching easier for the instructors.

Early literacy is everything a child need about reading and writing before he/she can read or write.

Letter knowledge:

To read words children have to understand that a word is made up of individual sounds

Examples:

a, b, c, d, e, f, g, h, i, j, k, l, m, n, o, p, q, r, s, t, u, v, w, x, y, z.

A child's journey towards literacy involves learning to speak, listen, read, understand, watch, paste, draw, and write. The foundation for building these skills begins at birth.

Early Literacy Activities

- Talking
- Singing
- Playing with sound
- Pasting
- Writing and drawing

These are good ways to set up a good literacy foundation.

<u>Important of Literacy</u>:

This is to help the young children get ready for school by working with them to develop early literacy and learning skills because strong reading skills form the basis of learning in all subjects. It is important to identify those who struggle with reading as early as possible.

Week 1: IDENTIFICATION OF SOUND "a – f"

Day 1

Reading of Sound with Objects "a –f"

Materials

- A tray
- 6 big flash cards i.e. a-apple, b-bat, c-cap, d-drum, e-egg, f-fish.

Presentation

- Bring out the 6 flash cards for the pupil to see.
- Invite the pupils to work with you.
- Assemble them to sit on a chair.
- Bring out the flash cards and read for the pupils.
- Tell the pupils to repeat the sounds after you.
- Allow the pupils to pass the sound flash cards round among themselves.
- Return the sound back to the tray.
- Dismiss the pupils from the chair.

Day 2

Reading of sound with objects a – f

a, b, c, d, e, f.

Materials

- A tray
- 6 big flash cards
- a-ant
- b-banana
- c-cup
- d-duck
- e-envelope
- f- flag

Presentation

- Bring out the 6 flash cards for the pupil to see
- Invite the pupils to work with you
- Assemble them to sit on a chair
- Bring out the flash cards and read for the pupils
- Tell the pupils to repeat the sounds after you.
- Allow the pupils to pass the sound flash cards round among themselves
- Return the sound back to the tray
- Dismiss the pupils from the chair.

Day 3

Reading of sound with objects a – f (2 objects/sound)

a, b, c, d, e, f.

Materials

- A rug
- 6 big flash cards

a- ant, arrow

b- banana, bat

c- cup, cap

Presentation

- Bring out the 6 flash cards for the pupil to see
- Invite the pupils and assemble them on the rug
- Instructor place the flash cards on the floor
- Raise each flash card up for the pupils to say the sound and objects, turn by turn.
- Place the flash cards back on the floor and call the pupil to pick the sound you call. i.e Tunde stand up and pick "b" as in banana.

Day 4

READING OF SOUND WITH OBJECTS A – F

a, b, c, d, e, f.6

Materials

- A rug
- 6 big flash cards

d-duck, drum

e-egg, envelope

f-fish, flag

Presentation

- Bring out the 6 flash cards for the pupil to see
- Invite the pupils and assemble them on the rug
- Director place the flash cards on the floor
- Raise each flash card up for the pupils to say the sound and objects, turn by turn.
- Place the flash cards back on the floor and call the pupil to pick the sound you call. i.e Tunde stand up and pick "d" as in duck.

Day 5

Materials

- A rug
- 12 big flash cards

a- ant, arrow
b- b- banana, bat
c- cup, cap
d- duck, drum
e- egg, envelope
f- fish, flag

Presentation

- Bring out the 12 flash cards for the pupil to see
- Invite the pupils and assemble them on the rug
- Raise the sounds up for the pupils to identify one by one
- Turn the flash card upside down on the rug
- Call each Pupil to pick a sound at random and identify the sound he/she picked.

WEEK 2: IDENTIFICATION OF SOUND "a"

Day 1

Reading of sound "a"

Materials

- 3 Flash cards ("a" as in apple, ant, arrow)
- Phonics bag.

Presentation

- Bring out the three flash cards.
- Place the cards on the table.
- Assemble the pupils together
- Read the sound and the object to the pupils and also ensure to show the body demonstration.
- Allow the pupils to pass the flash cards around.
- Return the flash cards to the phonics bag.
- Hang the bag back on the wall.

Day 2

Pasting Of Sound "A" On Worksheet

Materials:

- My Phonics worksheet
- Pelican card of "a" sound
- Water gum
- Tray
- Towel

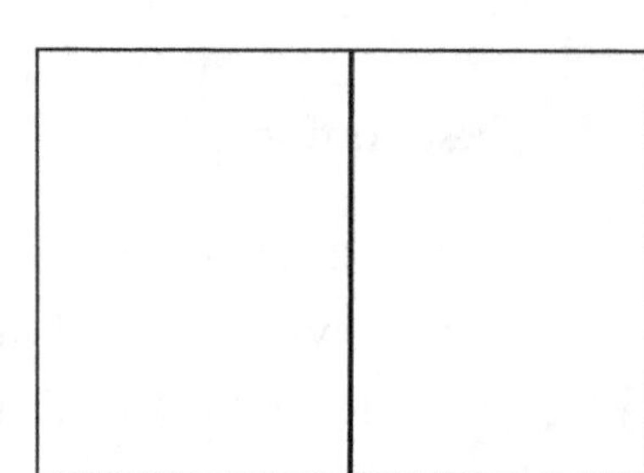

Presentation

- Bring out the required materials and place them on the table.
- Tell the pupils the name of the materials you have on the table.
- Call the pupils one by one to pick the "a" sound
- Provide them with a gum.
- Demonstrate to them how to wet the pelican card that has sound

"a'' written on it with gum

- Allow them all to wet the back of the sound with considerable amount of gum.

- Provide each pupil with their own Jolly phonics worksheet.
- Allow the pupils to paste the sound "a" on the provided worksheet.

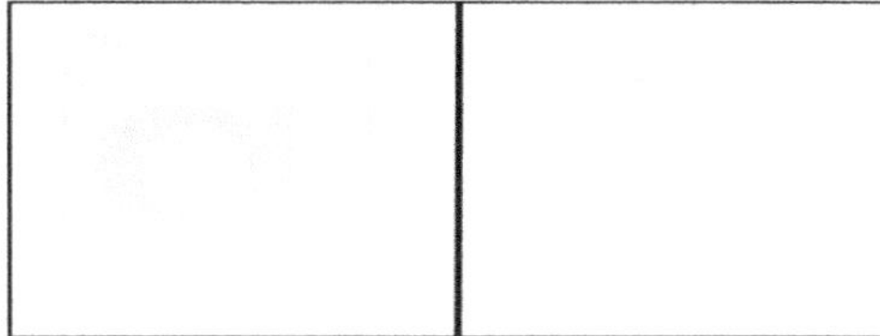

Paste "a" on the worksheet

Day 3

Pasting Of Sound on Object

Materials

-
- Creative reading worksheets
- Gum
- Cutout object of apple
- cutout of sound "a"
- Tray

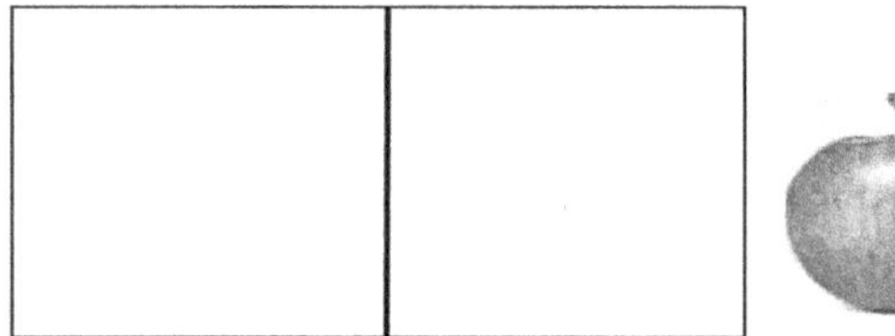

Presentation

- Bring out the required materials and place them on the table.
- Tell the pupils the name of the materials you have on the table.
- Call the pupils one by one to pick the "a" sound.
- Demonstrate to them how to wet the pelican card that has sound "a" written on it with gum.
- Allow them all to wet the back of the sound with considerable amount of gum and then paste it on the cutout object of apple.
- Bring out their worksheets and let them paste the object with sound on it.

Paste the cutout of sound "a" on the cutout object apple   Paste the cutout of the object apple with sound "a" on the worksheet

Day 4

Colouring Of Sound with Object

Materials

- Exercise book
- Jumbo Crayon
- A stamp
- Object stamp
- Stamp pad

Presentation

- Bring out the required materials and place them on the table.
- Invite one child at a time to work with.
- Place the exercise book, crayon, and the stamp pad on the table for the child.
- Stamp the sound and the object on the exercise book.
- Ask the pupil to point at the objects
- Give the pupil the blue crayon to color the "a" sound.
- Give the pupil the yellow crayon to color the object arrow.

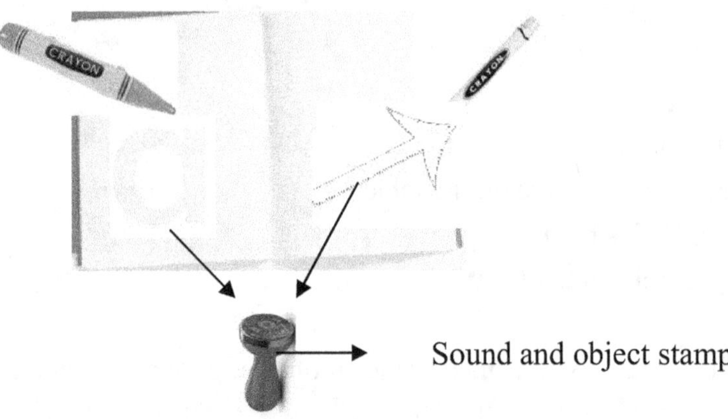

Sound and object stamp

Colour the sound with the blue crayon

Colour the object bat with the yellow crayon

Day 5

Pasting of sound with object "a" as in ant

Materials

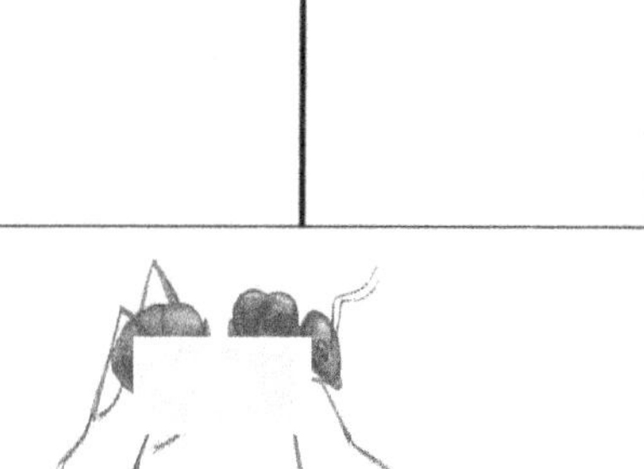

- Creative reading worksheets
- Gum
- Cutout of sound with object "a" as in ant
- Tray

Presentation

- Bring out the required materials and place them on the table.
- Tell the pupils the name of the materials you have on the table.
- Call the pupils one by one to pick the cutout of sound with object "a" as in ant
- Demonstrate to them how to wet the pelican card that has sound "a" and object ant with gum
- Allow them all to wet the back of the sound with object cutout with considerable amount of gum.
- Bring out their worksheets and let them paste the object with sound on it.

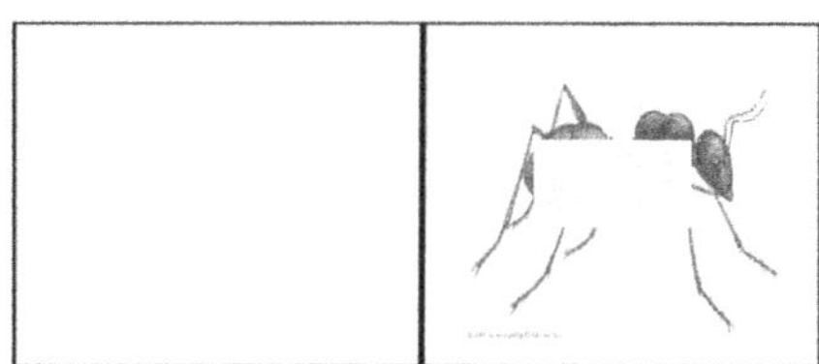

Paste the cutout of the object ant with sound "a" on the worksheet

<h1 style="text-align:center">WEEK 3 IDENTIFICATION OF SOUND "B"</h1>

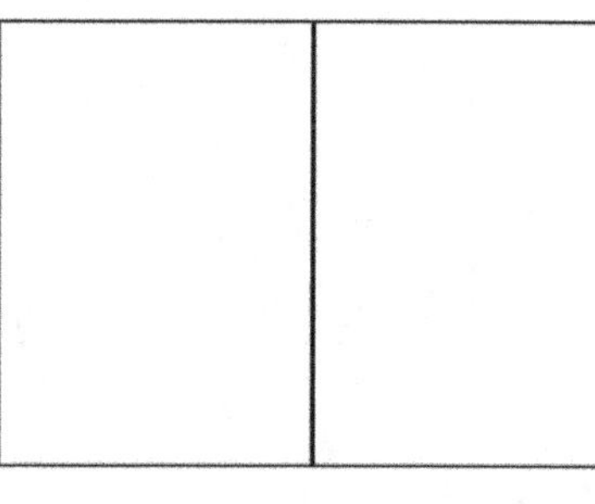

Day 1

Reading of Sound "b"

Materials

- 3 Flash cards ("b" as in bat, banana, butterfly)
- Phonics bag.

Presentation

- Bring out the three flash cards.
- Place the cards on the table.
- Assemble the pupils together
- Read the sound and the objects to the pupils and also ensure to show the body demonstration.
- Allow the pupils to pass the flash cards around.
- Return the flash cards to the phonics bag.
- Hang the bag back on the wall.

Day 2

Pasting of Sound "b" On Worksheet

Materials:

- My Phonics worksheet
- Pelican card of "b" sound
- Water gum
- Tray
- Towel
- Pelican card of "b" sound
- My Phonics worksheet

Presentation

- Bring out the required materials and place them on the table.
- Tell the pupils the name of the materials you have on the table.
- Call the pupils one by one to pick the "b" sound
- Provide them with a gum.
- Demonstrate to them how to wet the pelican card that has sound.
  "b" written on it with gum.
- Allow them all to wet the back of the sound with considerable amount of gum.
- Provide each pupil with their own Jolly phonics worksheet.
- Allow the pupils to paste the sound "b" on the provided worksheet.

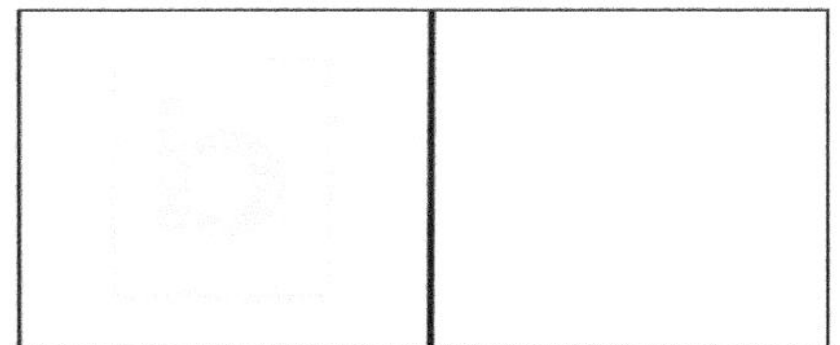

Paste the sound "b" on the worksheet

Day 3

Pasting of Sound on Object

Materials

- Creative reading worksheets
- Gum
- Cutout object of banana
- cutout of sound "b"
- Tray

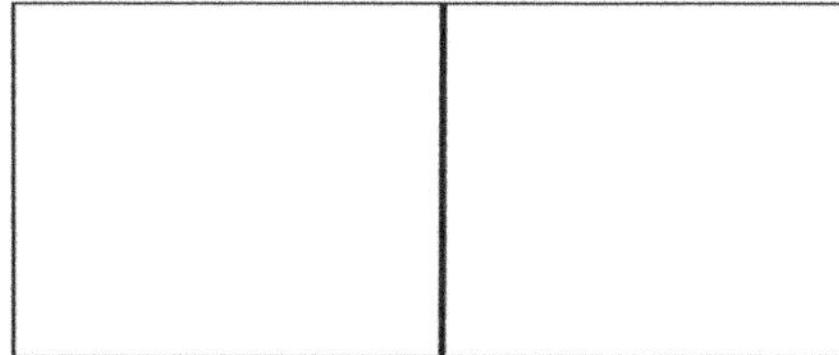

Presentation

- Bring out the required materials and place them on the table.
- Tell the pupils the name of the materials you have on the table.
- Call the pupils one by one to pick the "b" sound.
- Demonstrate to them how to wet the sound pelican card with gum.
- Allow them all to wet the back of the sound with considerable amount of gum and then paste it on the cutout object of banana.
- Bring out their worksheets and let them paste the object with sound on it.

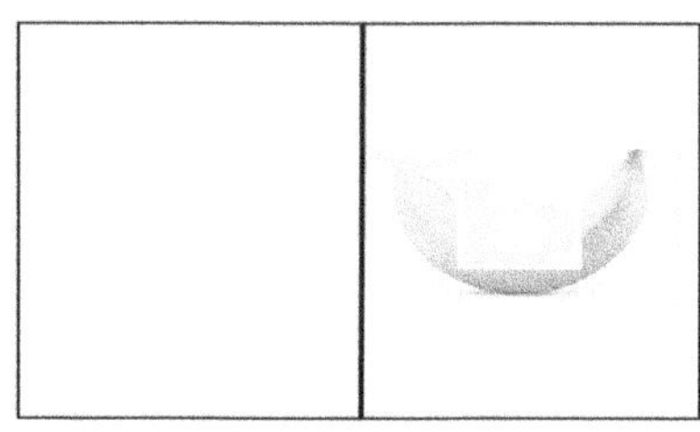

Paste the cutout of sound "b" on the cutout object banana

Paste the cutout of the object banana with sound "b" on the worksheet

Day 4

Colouring of Sound with Object

Materials

- Exercise book
- Jumbo Crayon
- A stamp
- Object stamp
- Stamp pad

Presentation

- Bring out the required materials and place them on the table.
- Invite one child at a time to work with.
- Place the exercise book, crayon, and the stamp pad on the table for the child.
- Stamp the sound and the object on the exercise book.
- Ask the pupil to point at the objects
- Give the pupil the blue crayon to color the "b" sound.
- Give the pupil the yellow crayon to color the object bat.

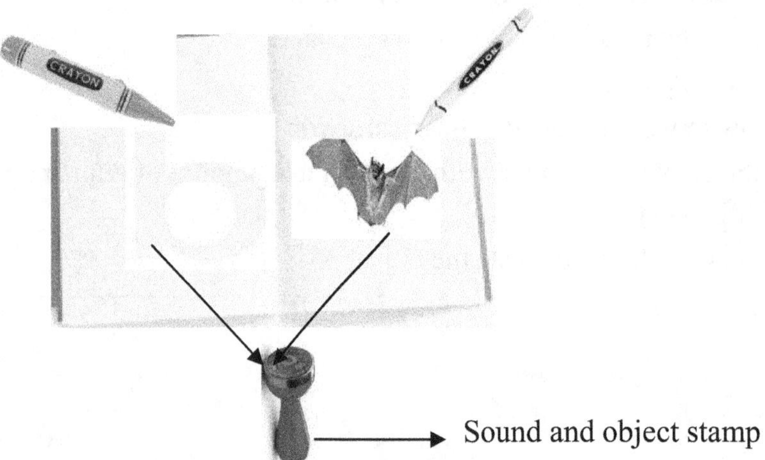

Colour the sound with the blue crayon

Colour the object bat with the yellow crayon

Day 5

Pasting of Sound with object "b" As in butterfly

Materials

- Creative reading worksheets
- Gum
- Cutout of sound with object "b" as in butterfly
- Tray

Presentation

- Bring out the required materials and place them on the table.
- Tell the pupils the name of the materials you have on the table.
- Call the pupils one by one to pick the cutout of sound with object "b" as in butterfly
- Demonstrate to them how to wet the sound pelican card with gum
- Allow them all to wet the back of the sound with object cutout with considerable amount of gum.
- Bring out their worksheets and let them paste the object with sound on it.

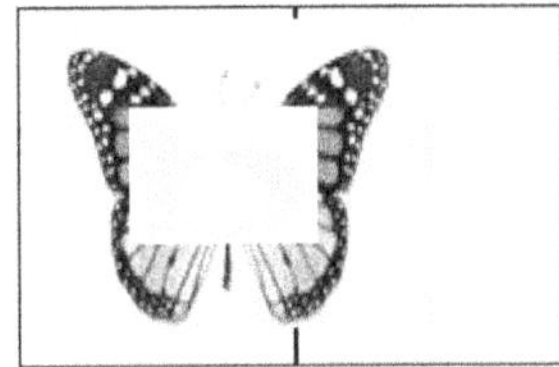

Paste the cutout of the object butterfly with sound "b" on the worksheet

Day 1

Reading of Sound "c"

Materials

- 3 Flash cards ("c" as in cup, cap clock,)
- Phonics bag.

Presentation

- Bring out the three flash cards.
- Place the cards on the table.
- Assemble the pupils together
- Read the sound and the object to the pupils and also ensure to show the body demonstration.
- Allow the pupils to pass the flash cards around.
- Return the flash cards to the phonics bag.
- Hang the bag back on the wall.

Day 2

Pasting of Sound "C" on Worksheet

Materials:

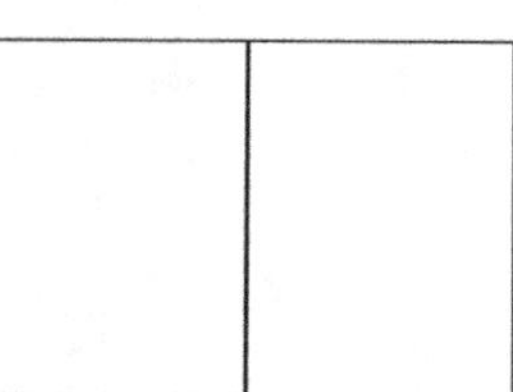

- My Phonics worksheet
- Pelican card of "c" sound
- Water gum
- Tray
- Towel

Presentation

- Bring out the required materials and place them on the table.
- Tell the pupils the name of the materials you have on the table.
- Call the pupils one by one to pick the "c" sound
- Provide them with a gum.
- Demonstrate to them how to wet the pelican card that has sound "c'' written on it with the gum.

- Allow them all to wet the back of the sound with considerable amount of gum.
- Provide each pupil with their own Jolly phonics worksheet.
- Allow the pupils to paste the sound "c" on the provided worksheet.

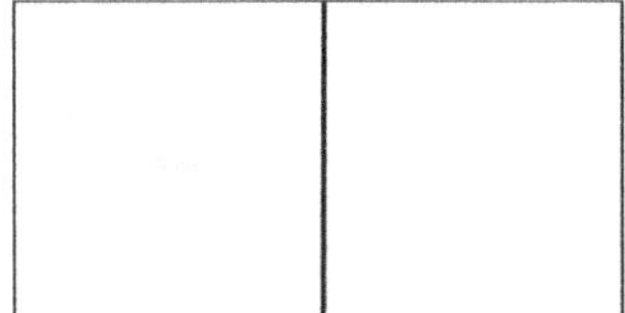

Paste the sound "c" on the provided worksheet.

Day 3

Pasting of Sound on Object

Materials

- Creative reading worksheets
- Gum
- Cutout object of clock
- cutout of sound "c"
- Tray

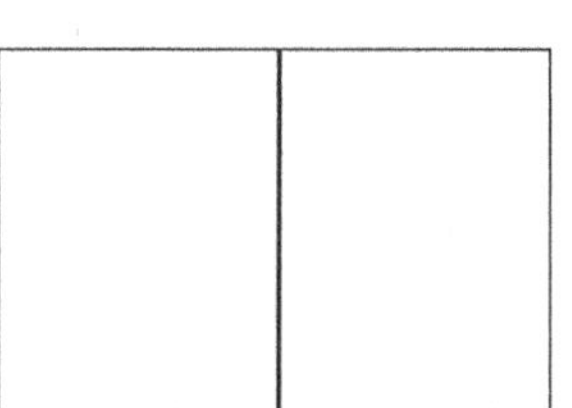

Worksheet

cutout of sound "c"   Cutout object of bat

Presentation

- Bring out the required materials and place them on the table.
- Tell the pupils the name of the materials you have on the table.
- Call the pupils one by one to pick the "c" sound
- Demonstrate to them how to wet the sound pelican card with gum.
- Allow them all to wet the back of the sound with considerable amount of gum and then paste it on the cutout object clock.
- Bring out their worksheets and let them paste the object with sound "c" on it.

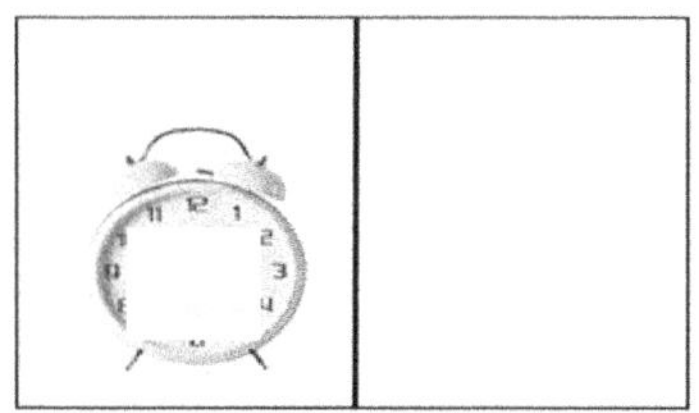

Paste the cutout of sound "c" on the cutout object clock   **Paste the cutout of the object clock with sound "c" on the worksheet**

Day 4

Colouring of Sound with Object

Materials

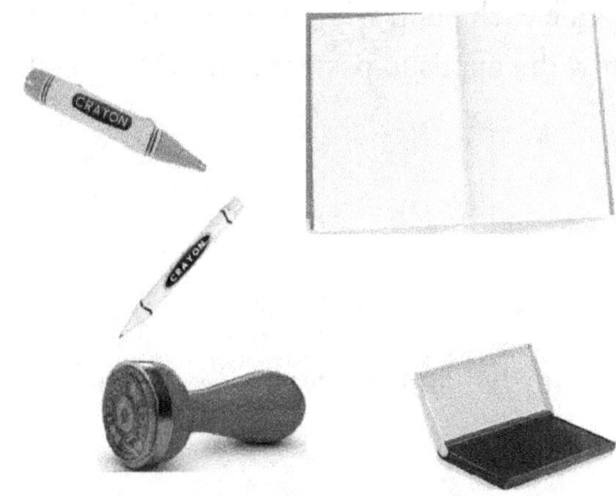

- Exercise book
- Jumbo Crayon
- A stamp

- Object stamp
- Stamp pad

Presentation

- Bring out the required materials and place them on the table.
- Invite one child at a time to work with.
- Place the exercise book, crayon, and the stamp pad on the table for the child.
- Stamp the sound and the object on the exercise book.
- Ask the pupil to point at the objects
- Give the pupil the blue crayon to color the "c" sound.
- Give the pupil the yellow crayon to color the object.

Colour the sound "c" with blue crayon

Colour the object cap with yellow crayon

Day 5

Pasting Of Sound with Object "c" As In clock

Materials

- Creative reading worksheets
- Gum
- Cutout of sound with object "c" as in clock
- Tray

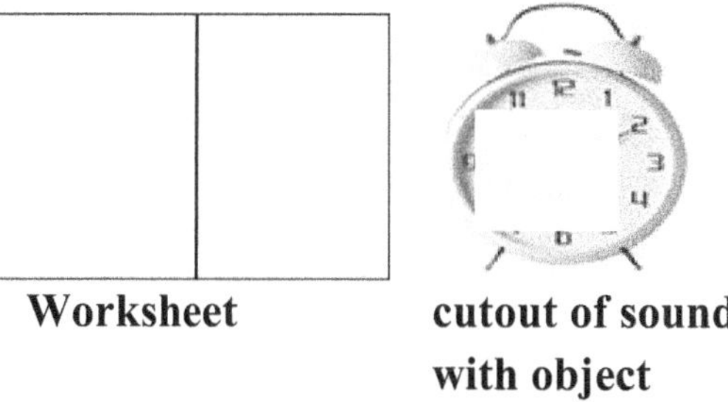

Worksheet   **cutout of sound with object**

Presentation

- Bring out the required materials and place them on the table.
- Tell the pupils the name of the materials you have on the table.
- Call the pupils one by one to pick the cutout of sound with object "c" as in clock
- Demonstrate to them how to wet the sound pelican card with gum
- Allow them all to wet the back of the sound with object cutout with considerable amount of gum.
- Bring out their worksheets and let them paste the object with sound on it.

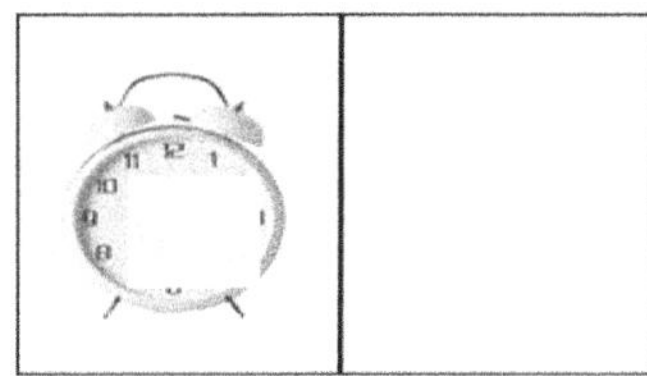

Paste the cutout of the object clock with sound "c" on the worksheet

Day 1

Reading of Sound "d"

Materials

- 3 Flash cards ("d" as in duck, drum, door)
- Phonics bag.

Presentation

- Bring out the three flash cards.
- Place the cards on the table.
- Assemble the pupils together
- Read the sound and the object to the pupils and also ensure to show the body demonstration.
- Allow the pupils to pass the flash cards around.
- Return the flash cards to the phonics bag.
- Hang the bag back on the wall.

Day 2

Pasting of Sound "d" on Worksheet

Materials:

- My Phonics worksheet
- Pelican card of "d" sound
- Water gum
- Tray
- Towel

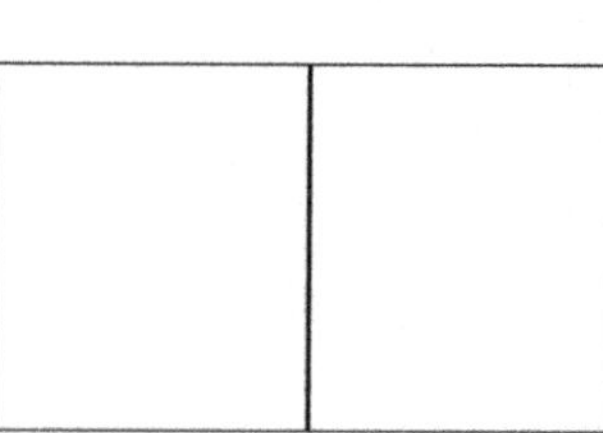

Presentation

- Bring out the required materials and place them on the table.
- Tell the pupils the name of the materials you have on the table.
- Call the pupils one by one to pick the "d" sound
- Provide them with a gum.
- Demonstrate to them how to wet the pelican card that has sound "d'' written on it with gum.
- Allow them all to wet the back of the sound with considerable amount of gum.
- Provide each pupil with their own Jolly phonics worksheet.
- Allow the pupils to paste the sound "d" on the provided worksheet.

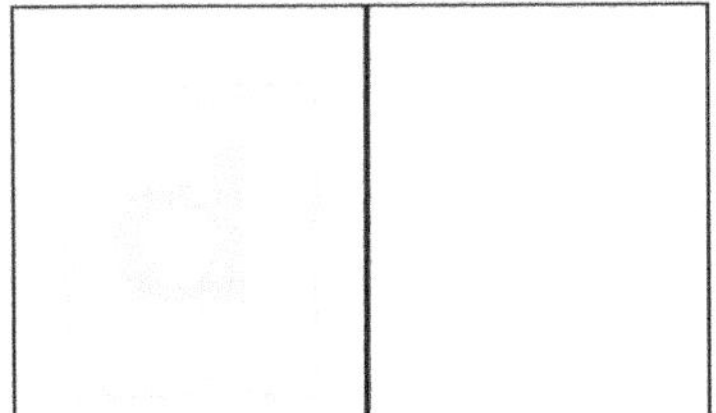

Paste the sound "d" on the worksheet

Day 3

Pasting of Sound on Object

Materials

- Creative reading worksheets
- Gum
- Cutout object of door
- cutout of sound "d"
- Tray

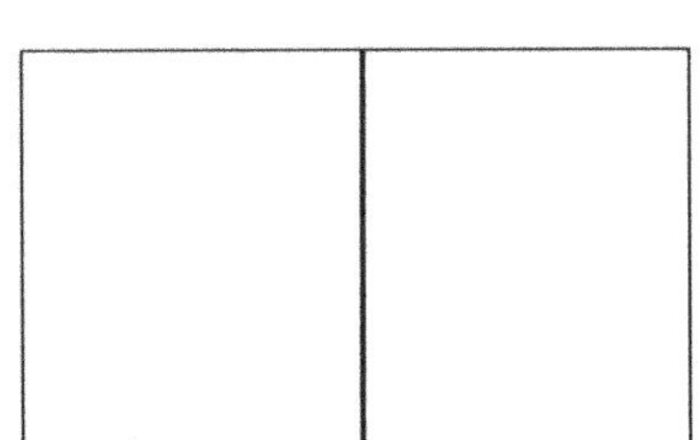

Presentation

- Bring out the required materials and place them on the table.
- Tell the pupils the name of the materials you have on the table.
- Call the pupils one by one to pick the "d" sound
- Demonstrate to them how to wet the sound pelican card with gum
- Allow them all to wet the back of the sound with considerable amount of gum and then paste it on the cutout object of door.
- Bring out their worksheets and let them paste the object with sound on it.

Paste the cutout of sound "d" on the cutout object door

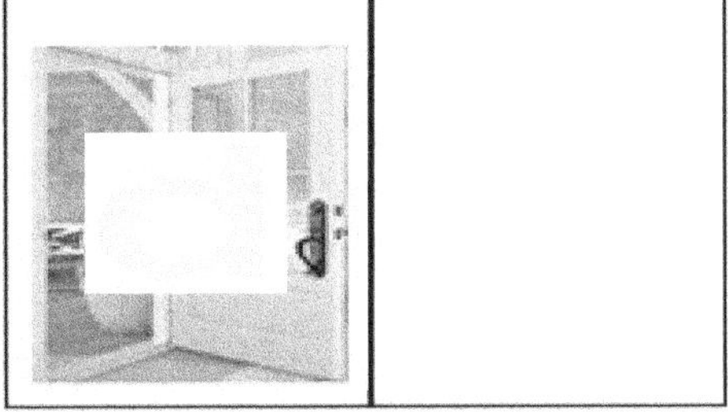

Paste the cutout of the object (door) with sound "d" on the worksheet

Day 4

Colouring of Sound with Object

Materials

- Exercise book
- Jumbo Crayon
- A stamp
- Object stamp of drum

- Stamp pad

Presentation

- Bring out the required materials and place them on the table.
- Invite one child at a time to work with.
- Place the exercise book, crayon, and the stamp pad on the table for the child.
- Stamp the sound and the object on the exercise book.
- Ask the pupil to point at the objects
- Give the pupil the blue crayon to color the "d" sound.
- Give the pupil the yellow crayon to color the object.

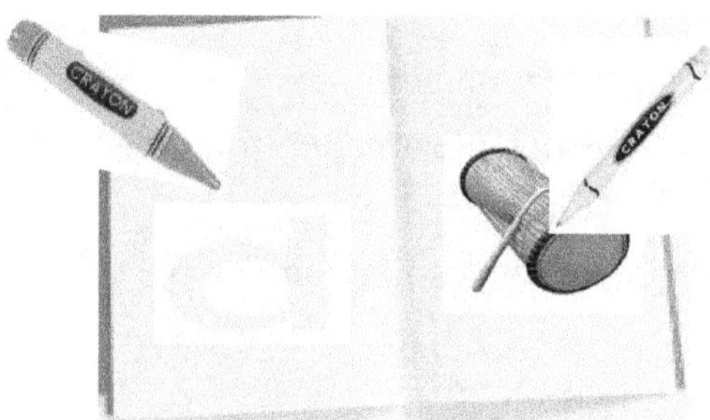

Colour the sound "d" with blue crayon

Colour the object drum with yellow crayon

Day 5

Pasting of Sound with object "d" as in duck

Materials

- Creative reading worksheets
- Gum
- Cutout of sound with object "d" as in duck.
- Tray

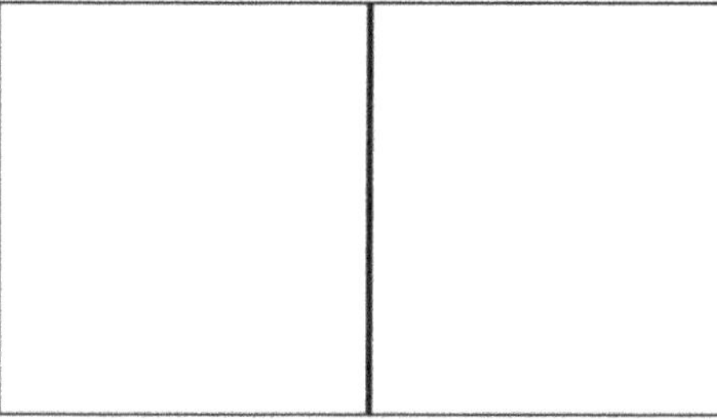 

Presentation

- Bring out the required materials and place them on the table.
- Tell the pupils the name of the materials you have on the table.
- Call the pupils one by one to pick the cutout of sound with object "d" as in duck
- Demonstrate to them how to wet the sound's pelican card with gum
- Allow them all to wet the back of the sound with object cutout with considerable amount of gum.
- Bring out their worksheets and let them paste the object with sound on it.

Paste the object with sound on the worksheet

WEEK 6 IDENTIFICATION OF SOUND "e"

Day 1

Reading of Sound "e"

Materials

- 3 Flash cards ("e" as in egg, envelope, elephant)
- Phonics bag.

Presentation

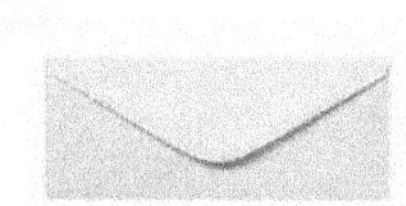

- Bring out the three flash cards.
- Place the cards on the table.
- Assemble the pupils together
- Read the sound and the object to the pupils and also ensure to show the body demonstration.
- Allow the pupils to pass the flash cards around.
- Return the flash cards to the phonics bag.
- Hang the bag back on the wall.

Day 2

Pasting of Sound "e" on Worksheet

Materials:

- My Phonics worksheet
- Pelican card of "e" sound
- Water gum
- Tray
- Towel

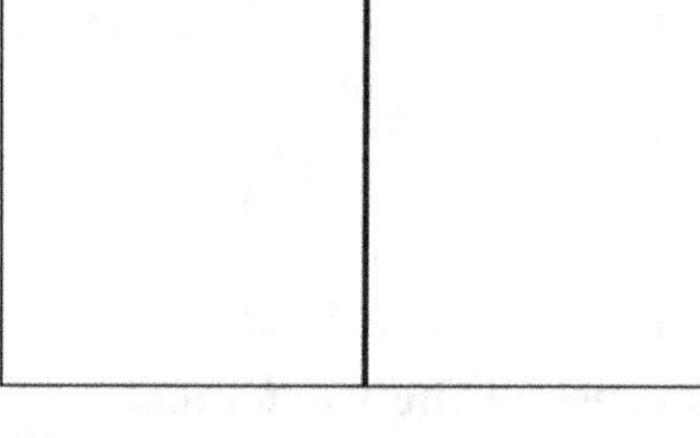

Presentation

- Bring out the required materials and place them on the table.
- Tell the pupils the name of the materials you have on the table.
- Call the pupils one by one to pick the "e" sound
- Provide them with a gum.
- Demonstrate to them how to wet the sound pelican card with gum
- Allow them all to wet the back of the sound with considerable amount of gum.
- Provide each pupil with their own Jolly phonics worksheet.
- Allow the pupils to paste the sound "e" on the provided worksheet.

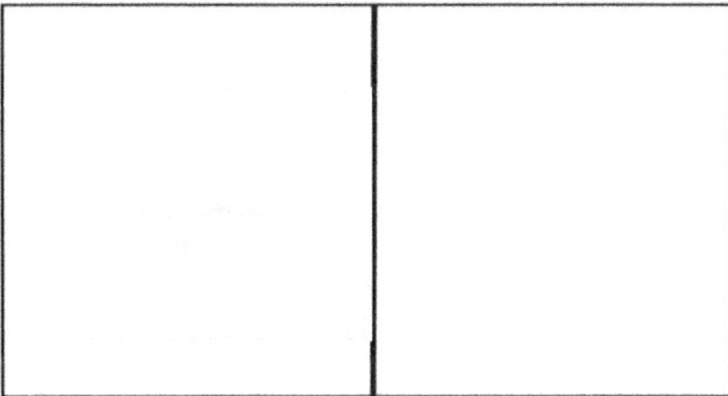

Paste the sound "e" Pelican card on the worksheet

Day 3

Pasting of Sound "e" on Object

Materials

- Creative reading worksheets
- Gum
- Cutout object of egg
- cutout of sound "e"
- Tray

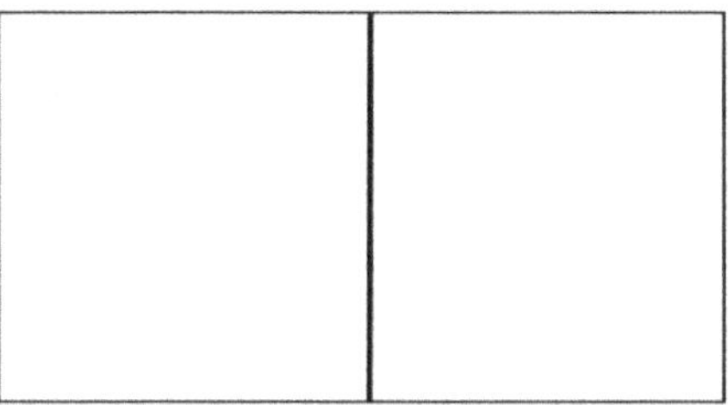

Presentation

- Bring out the required materials and place them on the table.
- Tell the pupils the name of the materials you have on the table.
- Call the pupils one by one to pick the "e" sound
- Demonstrate to them how to wet the sound pelican card with gum
- Allow them all to wet the back of the sound with considerable amount of gum and then paste it on the cutout object of door.
- Bring out their worksheets and let them paste the object with sound on it.

Paste the cutout of sound "e" on the object egg

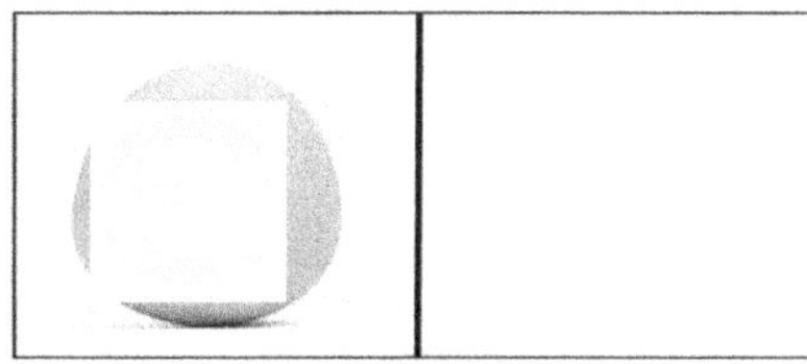

Paste the object egg with sound "e" on the worksheet

Day 4

Colouring of Sound with Object

Materials

- Exercise book
- Jumbo Crayon
- A stamp
- Object stamp
- Stamp pad

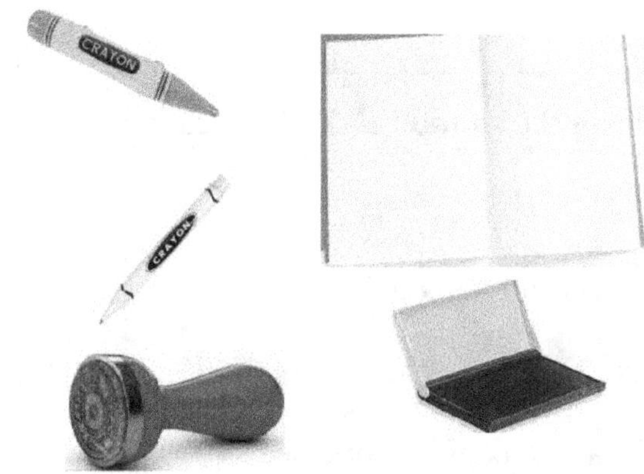

Presentation

- Bring out the required materials and place them on the table.
- Invite one child at a time to work with.
- Place the exercise book, crayon, and the stamp pad on the table for the child.
- Stamp the sound and the object on the exercise book.
- Ask the pupil to point at the objects
- Give the pupil the blue crayon to color the "e" sound.
- Give the pupil the yellow crayon to color the object.

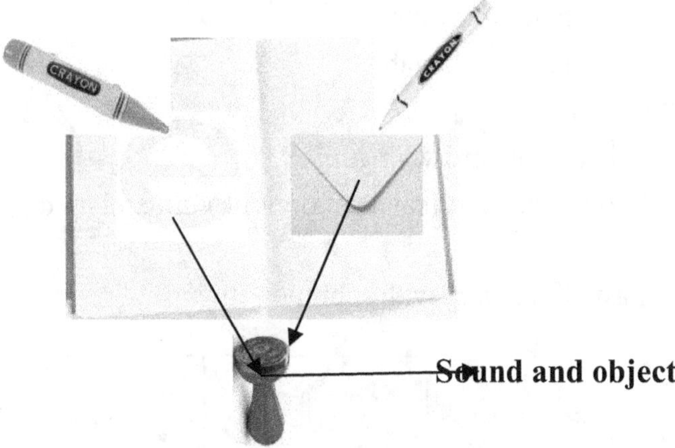

Colour the sound "e" in the exercise book with blue crayon

Colour the object envelope in the exercise book with yellow crayon.

Day 5

Pasting of Sound with Object "e" As In Elephant

Materials

- Creative reading worksheets
- Gum
- Cutout of sound with object "e" as in elephant
- Tray

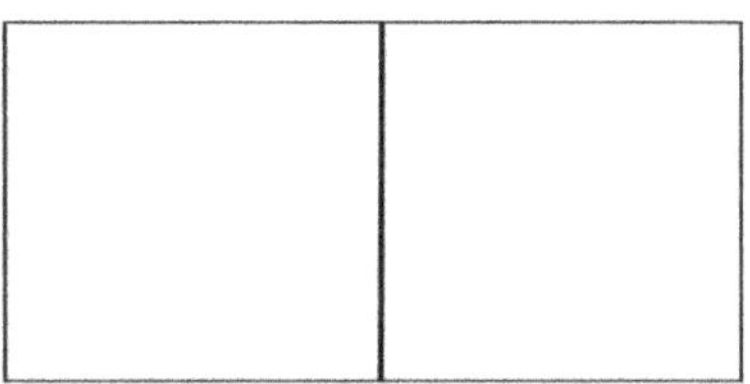 

Presentation

- Bring out the required materials and place them on the table.
- Tell the pupils the name of the materials you have on the table.
- Call the pupils one by one to pick the cutout of sound with object "e" as in elephant
- Demonstrate to them how to wet the sound pelican card with gum
- Allow them all to wet the back of the sound with object cutout with considerable amount of gum.
- Bring out their worksheets and let them paste the object with sound on it.

Paste the object with sound on the worksheet

WEEK 7: IDENTIFICATION OF SOUND "f"

Day 1

Reading of Sound "f"

Materials

- 3 Flash cards ("f" as in flag, fish, fork)
- Phonics bag.

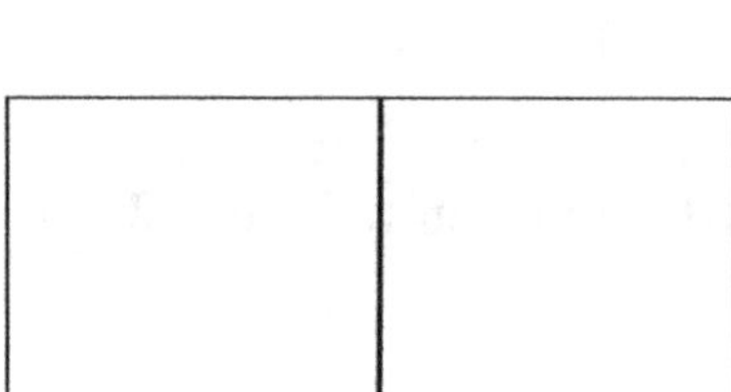

Presentation

- Bring out the three flash cards.
- Place the cards on the table.
- Assemble the pupils together
- Read the sound and the object to the pupils and also ensure to show the body demonstration.
- Allow the pupils to pass the flash cards around.
- Return the flash cards to the phonics bag.
- Hang the bag back on the wall.

Day 2

Pasting of Sound "f" on Worksheet

Materials:

- My Phonics worksheet
- Pelican card of "f" sound
- Water gum
- Tray
- Towel

Presentation

- Bring out the required materials and place them on the table.
- Tell the pupils the name of the materials you have on the table.
- Call the pupils one by one to pick the "f" sound
- Provide them with a gum.
- Demonstrate to them how to wet the sound pelican card with gum
- Allow them all to wet the back of the sound with considerable amount of gum.
- Provide each pupil with their own Jolly phonics worksheet.
- Allow the pupils to paste the sound "f" on the provided worksheet.

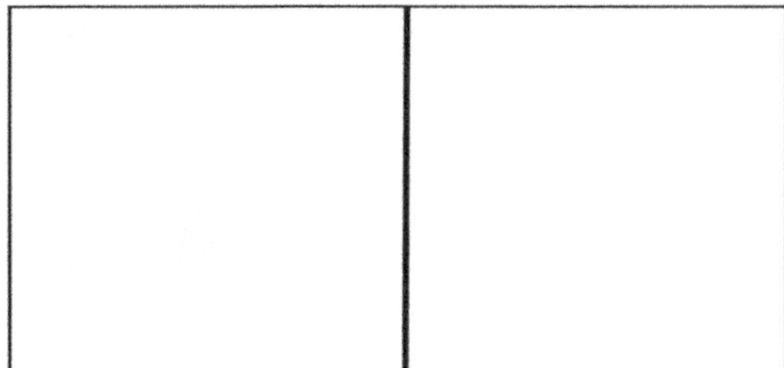

Paste the sound "f" Pelican card on the worksheet

Day 3

Pasting of Sound "f" on Object

Materials

- Creative reading worksheets
- Gum
- Cutout object of flag
- cutout of sound "f"
- Tray

Presentation

- Bring out the required materials and place them on the table.
- Tell the pupils the name of the materials you have on the table.
- Call the pupils one by one to pick the "f" sound
- Demonstrate to them how to wet the sound pelican card with gum
- Allow them all to wet the back of the sound with considerable amount of gum and then paste it on the cutout object of flag.
- Bring out their worksheets and let them paste the object with sound on it.

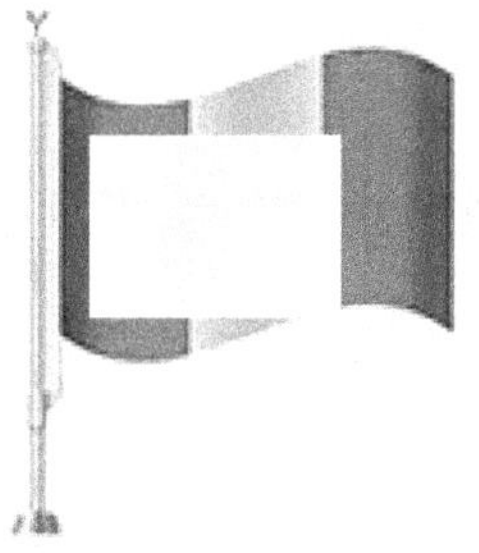

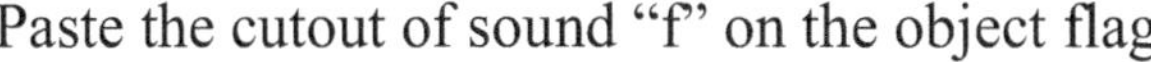

Paste the cutout of sound "f" on the object flag

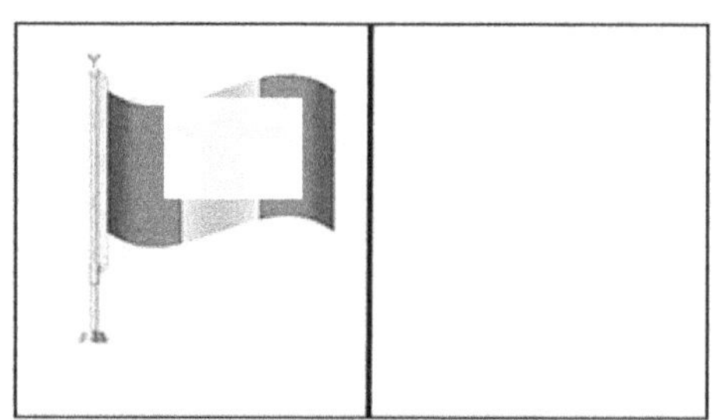

Paste the object flag with sound "f", on the worksheet

Day 4

Colouring of Sound with Object

Materials

- Exercise book
- Jumbo Crayon
- A stamp
- Object stamp
- Stamp pad

Presentation

- Bring out the required materials and place them on the table.
- Invite one child at a time to work with.
- Place the exercise book, crayon, and the stamp pad on the table for the child.
- Stamp the sound and the object on the exercise book.
- Ask the pupil to point at the objects
- Give the pupil the blue crayon to color the "f" sound.
- Give the pupil the yellow crayon to color the object fish.

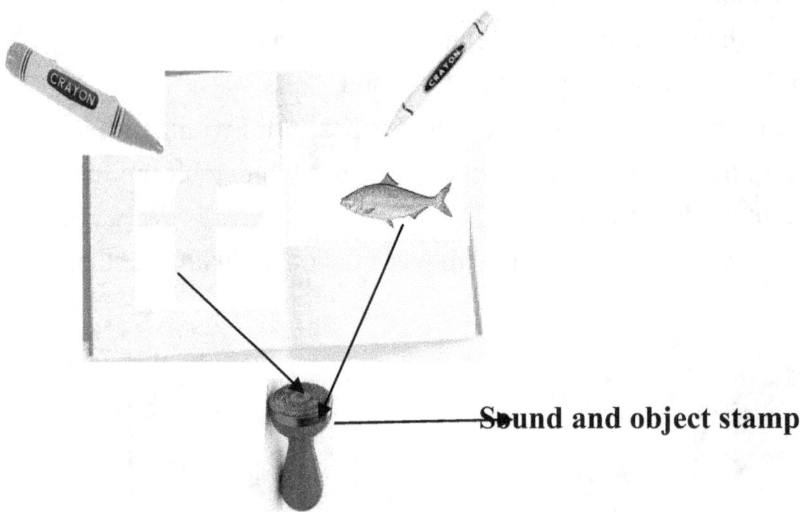

Colour the sound "g" in the exercise book with blue crayon

Colour the object girl in the exercise book with yellow crayon

Day 5

Pasting of sound with object "f" as in fork

Materials

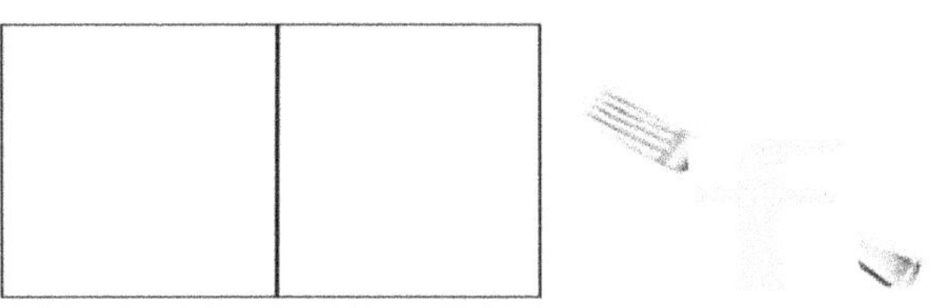

- Creative reading worksheets
- Gum
- Cutout of sound with object "f" as in fork
- Tray

Presentation

- Bring out the required materials and place them on the table.
- Tell the pupils the name of the materials you have on the table.
- Call the pupils one by one to pick the cutout of sound with object "f" as in fork
- Demonstrate to them how to wet the sound's pelican card with gum
- Allow them all to wet the back of the sound with object cutout with considerable amount of gum.
- Bring out their worksheets and let them paste the object, fork with sound on it.

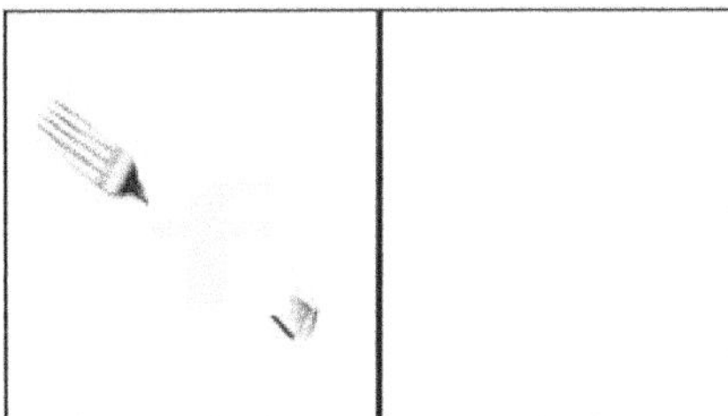

Paste the object with sound on the worksheet

WEEK 8 IDENTIFICATION OF SOUND "g"

Day 1

Reading of Sound "g"

Materials

- 3 Flash cards ("g" as in girl, gate, goose)
- Phonics bag.

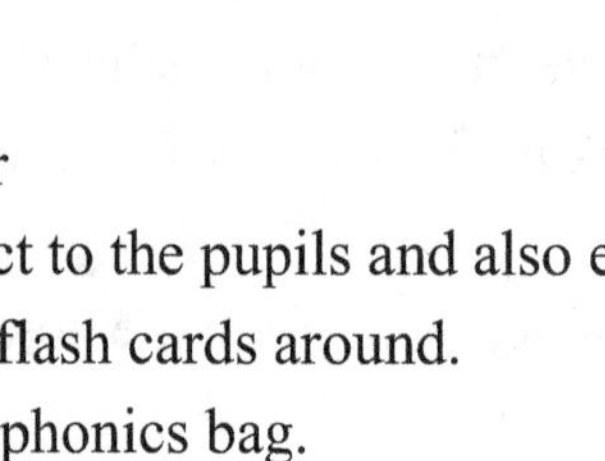

Presentation

- Bring out the three flash cards.
- Place the cards on the table.
- Assemble the pupils together
- Read the sound and the object to the pupils and also ensure to show the body demonstration.
- Allow the pupils to pass the flash cards around.
- Return the flash cards to the phonics bag.
- Hang the bag back on the wall.

Day 2

Pasting of Sound "g" on Worksheet

Materials:

- My Phonics worksheet
- Pelican card of "g" sound
- Water gum
- Tray

Presentation

- Bring out the required materials and place them on the table.
- Tell the pupils the name of the materials you have on the table.
- Call the pupils one by one to pick the "g" sound
- Provide them with a gum.
- Demonstrate to them how to wet the sound pelican card with gum
- Allow them all to wet the back of the sound with considerable amount of gum.
- Provide each pupil with their own Jolly phonics worksheet.
- Allow the pupils to paste the sound "g" on the provided worksheet.

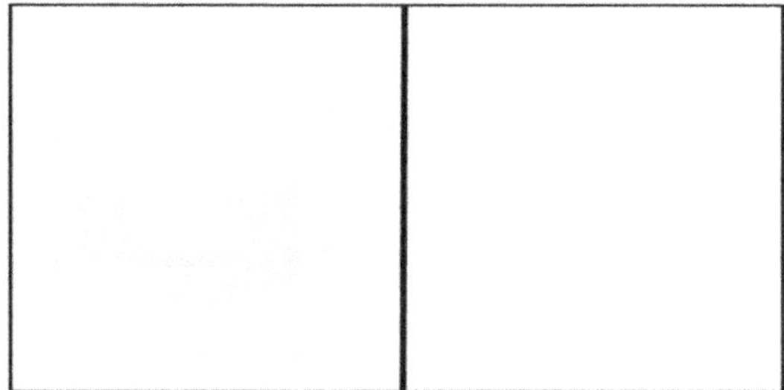

Paste the sound "g" Pelican card on the worksheet

Day 3

Pasting of Sound on Object

Materials

- Creative reading worksheets
- Gum
- Cutout object of goose
- cutout of sound "g"
- Tray

Presentation

- Bring out the required materials and place them on the table.
- Tell the pupils the name of the materials you have on the table.
- Call the pupils one by one to pick the "g" sound
- Demonstrate to them how to wet the sound pelican card with gum
- Allow them all to wet the back of the sound with considerable amount of gum and then paste it on the cutout object of goose.
- Bring out their worksheets and let them paste the object with sound on it.

Paste the cutout of sound "g" on the object goose

Paste the object goose with sound "g" on the worksheet

Day 4

Colouring of Sound with Object

Materials

- Exercise book
- Jumbo Crayon
- A stamp
- Object stamp
- Stamp pad

Presentation

- Bring out the required materials and place them on the table.
- Invite one child at a time to work with.
- Place the exercise book, crayon, and the stamp pad on the table for the child.
- Stamp the sound and the object on the exercise book.
- Ask the pupil to point at the objects
- Give the pupil the blue crayon to color the "g" sound.
- Give the pupil the yellow crayon to color the object.

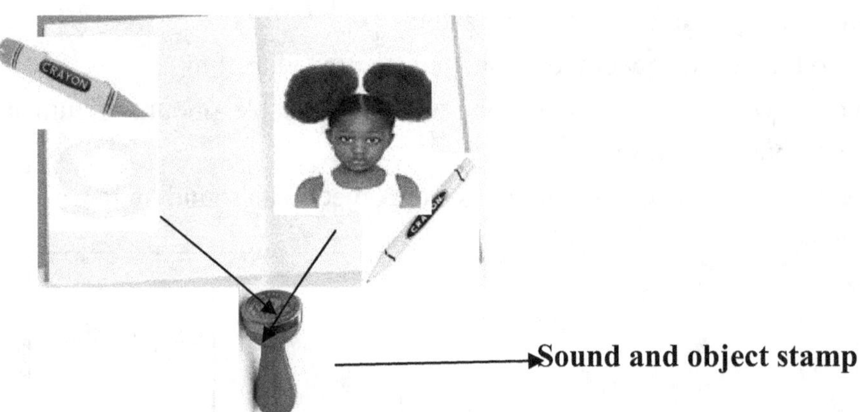

Colour the sound "g" in the exercise book with blue crayon

Colour the object girl in the exercise book with yellow crayon

Day 5

Pasting of Sound with Object "g" as in goose

Materials

- Creative reading worksheets
- Gum
- Cutout of sound with object "g" as in goose
- Tray

Presentation

- Bring out the required materials and place them on the table.
- Tell the pupils the name of the materials you have on the table.
- Call the pupils one by one to pick the cutout of sound with object "g" as in goose.
- Demonstrate to them how to wet the sound's pelican card with gum.
- Allow them all to wet the back of the sound with object cutout with considerable amount of gum.
- Bring out their worksheets and let them paste the object with sound on it.

Paste the object with sound on the worksheet

<h1 style="text-align:center">WEEK 9 IDENTIFICATION OF SOUND "h"</h1>

Day 1

Reading of Sound "h"

- 3 Flash cards ("h" as in hat, hen, house)
- Phonics bag.

Presentation

- Bring out the three flash cards.
- Place the cards on the table.
- Assemble the pupils together
- Read the sound and the object to the pupils and also ensure to show the body demonstration.
- Allow the pupils to pass the flash cards around.
- Return the flash cards to the phonics bag.
- Hang the bag back on the wall.

Day 2

Pasting of Sound "h" on Worksheet

Materials:

- My Phonics worksheet
- Pelican card of "h" sound
- Water gum
- Tray
- Towel

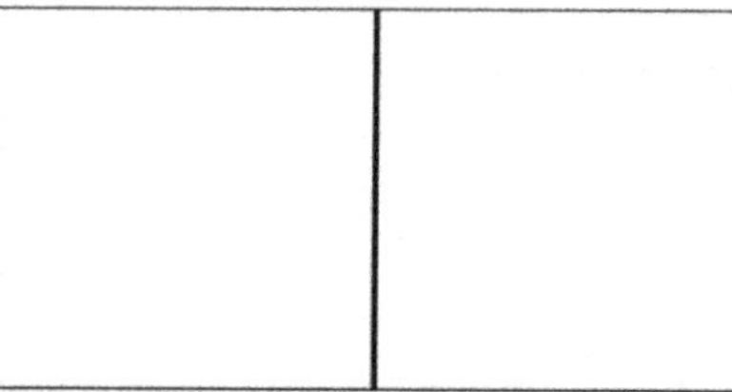

Presentation

- Bring out the required materials and place them on the table.
- Tell the pupils the name of the materials you have on the table.
- Call the pupils one by one to pick the "h" sound
- Provide them with a gum.
- Demonstrate to them how to wet the sound pelican card with gum
- Allow them all to wet the back of the sound with considerable amount of gum.
- Provide each pupil with their own Jolly phonics worksheet.
- Allow the pupils to paste the sound "h" on the provided worksheet.

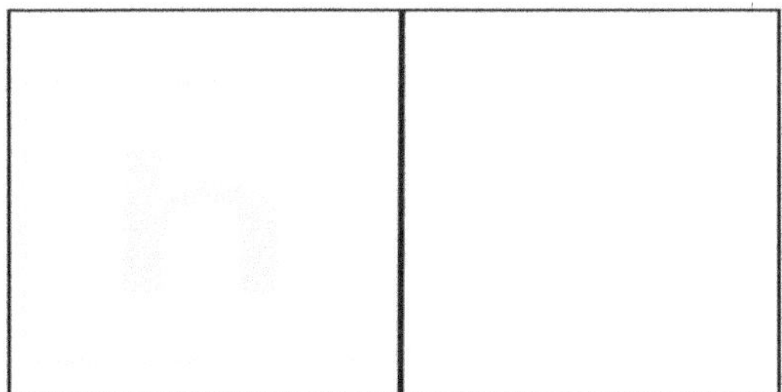

Paste the sound "h" Pelican card on the worksheet

Day 3

Pasting of Sound on Object

Materials

- Creative reading worksheets
- Gum
- Cutout object of hat
- cutout of sound "h"
- Tray

Presentation

- Bring out the required materials and place them on the table.
- Tell the pupils the name of the materials you have on the table.
- Call the pupils one by one to pick the "h" sound
- Demonstrate to them how to wet the sound pelican card with gum
- Allow them all to wet the back of the sound with considerable amount of gum and then paste it on the cutout object of hat.
- Bring out their worksheets and let them paste the object with sound on it.

Paste the cutout of sound "h" on the object hat

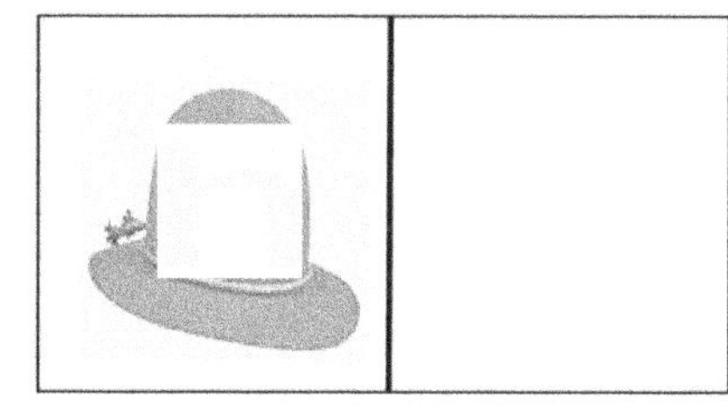

Paste the object hat with sound "h" on the worksheet

Day 4

Colouring of Sound with Object

Materials

- Exercise book
- Jumbo Crayon
- A stamp
- Object stamp
- Stamp pad

Presentation

- Bring out the required materials and place them on the table.
- Invite one child at a time to work with.
- Place the exercise book, crayon, and the stamp pad on the table for the child.
- Stamp the sound and the object on the exercise book.
- Ask the pupil to point at the objects
- Give the pupil the blue crayon to color the "h" sound.
- Give the pupil the yellow crayon to color the object.

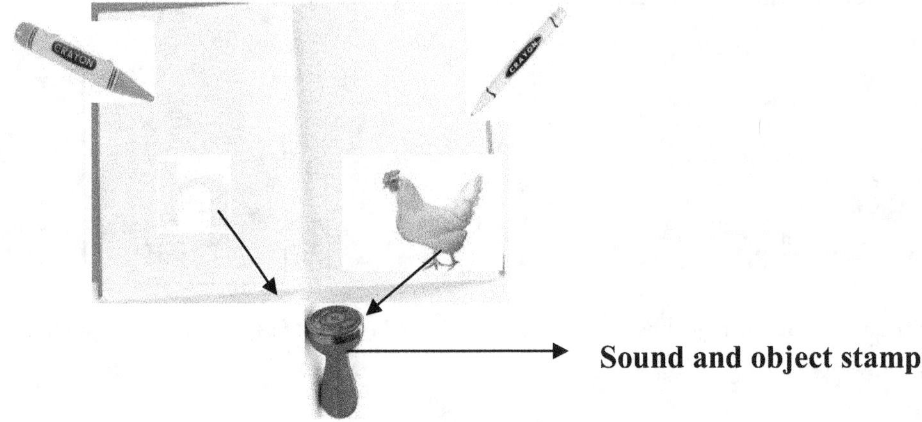

Colour the sound "h" in the exercise book with blue crayon

Colour the object hen in the exercise book with yellow crayon

Day 5

Pasting of Sound with Object "h" s in house

Materials

- Creative reading worksheets
- Gum
- Cutout of sound with object "h" as in house.
- Tray

Presentation

- Bring out the required materials and place them on the table.
- Tell the pupils the name of the materials you have on the table.
- Call the pupils one by one to pick the cutout of sound with object "h" as in HOUSE.
- Demonstrate to them how to wet the sound pelican card with gum.
- Allow them all to wet the back of the sound with object cutout with considerable amount of gum.
- Bring out their worksheets and let them paste the object with sound on it.

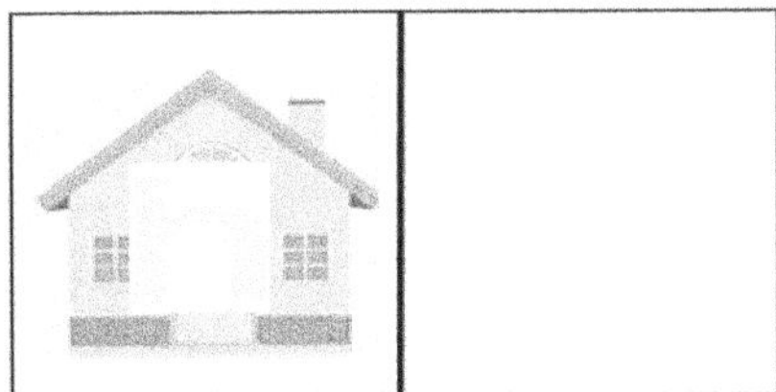

Paste the object with sound on the worksheet

WEEK 19 IDENTIFICATION OF SOUND "i"

Day 1

Reading of Sound "i"

Materials

- 3 Flash cards ("i" as in ink, ice, ice cream)
- Phonics bag.

Presentation

- Bring out the three flash cards.
- Place the cards on the table.
- Assemble the pupils together
- Read the sound and the object to the pupils and also ensure to show the body demonstration.
- Allow the pupils to pass the flash cards around.
- Return the flash cards to the phonics bag.
- Hang the bag back on the wall.

Day 2

Pasting of Sound "i" on Worksheet

Materials:

- My Phonics worksheet
- Pelican card of "i" sound
- Water gum
- Tray
- Towel

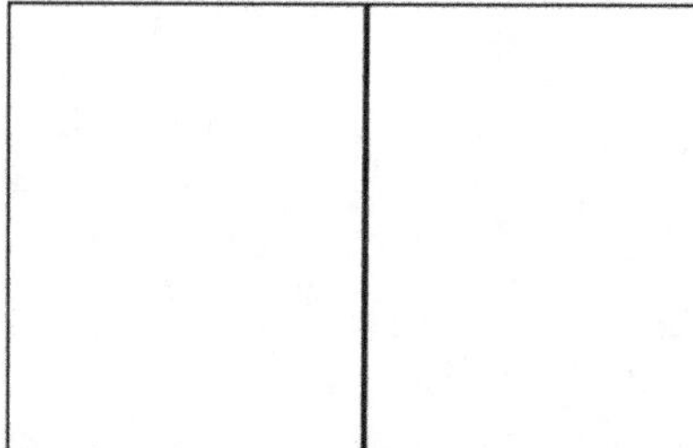

Presentation

- Bring out the required materials and place them on the table.
- Tell the pupils the name of the materials you have on the table.
- Call the pupils one by one to pick the "i" sound
- Provide them with a gum.
- Demonstrate to them how to wet the sound pelican card with gum
- Allow them all to wet the back of the sound with considerable amount of gum.

- Provide each pupil with their own Jolly phonics worksheet.
- Allow the pupils to paste the sound "i" on the provided worksheet.

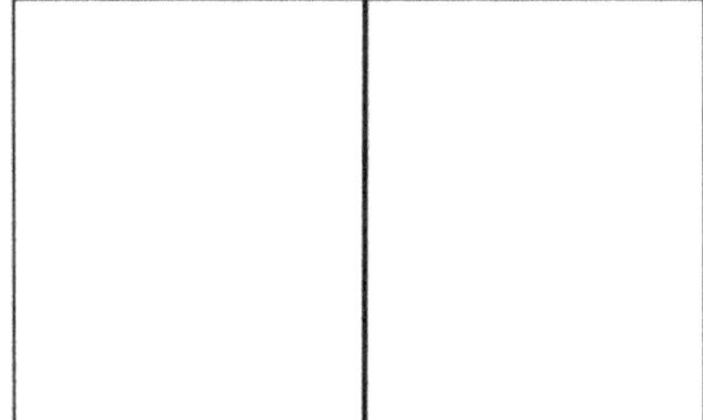

Paste the sound "i" Pelican card on the worksheet

Day 3

Pasting of Sound on Object

Materials

- Creative reading worksheets
- Gum
- Cutout object of ink
- cutout of sound "i"
- Tray

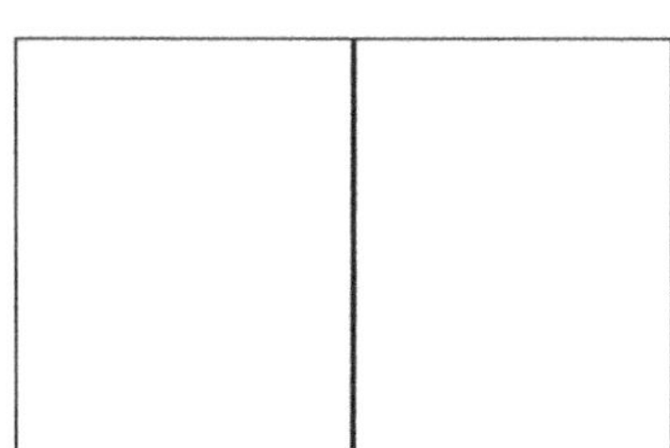

Presentation
- Bring out the required materials and place them on the table.
- Tell the pupils the name of the materials you have on the table.
- Call the pupils one by one to pick the "i" sound
- Demonstrate to them how to wet the sound pelican card with gum
- Allow them all to wet the back of the sound with considerable amount of gum and then paste it on the cutout object of ink.
- Bring out their worksheets and let them paste the object with sound on it.

Paste the cutout of sound "i" on the object ink

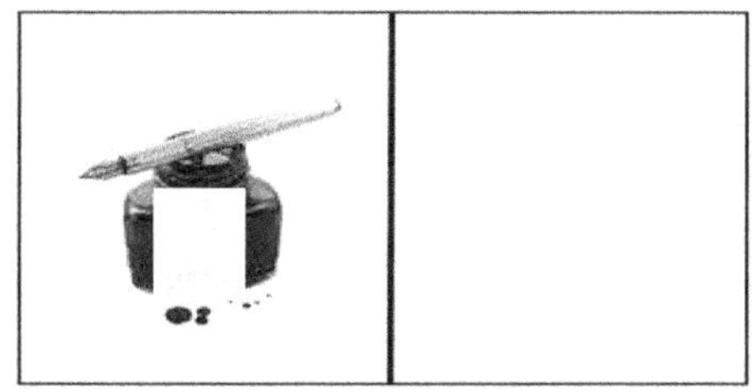

paste the object, ink with sound " i" on the worksheet

Day 4

Colouring of Sound with Object

Materials

- Exercise book
- Jumbo Crayon
- A stamp
- Object stamp
- Stamp pad

Presentation

- Bring out the required materials and place them on the table.
- Invite one child at a time to work with.
- Place the exercise book, crayon, and the stamp pad on the table for the child.
- Stamp the sound and the object on the exercise book.
- Ask the pupil to point at the objects
- Give the pupil the blue crayon to color the "i" sound.
- Give the pupil the yellow crayon to color the object.

Object stamp

Colour the sound "i" in the exercise book with blue crayon

Colour the object ice cream in the exercise book with yellow crayon

Day 5

Pasting of Sound with Object "i" as ink

Materials

- Creative reading worksheets
- Gum
- Cutout of sound with object "i" as in ink.
- Tray

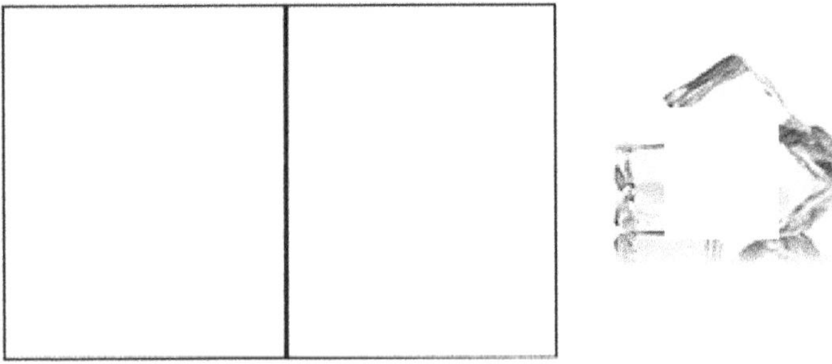

Presentation

- Bring out the required materials and place them on the table.
- Tell the pupils the name of the materials you have on the table.
- Call the pupils one by one to pick the cutout of sound with object "i" as in ice.
- Demonstrate to them how to wet the sound pelican card with gum.
- Allow them all to wet the back of the sound with object cutout with considerable amount of gum.
- Bring out their worksheets and let them paste the object with sound on it.

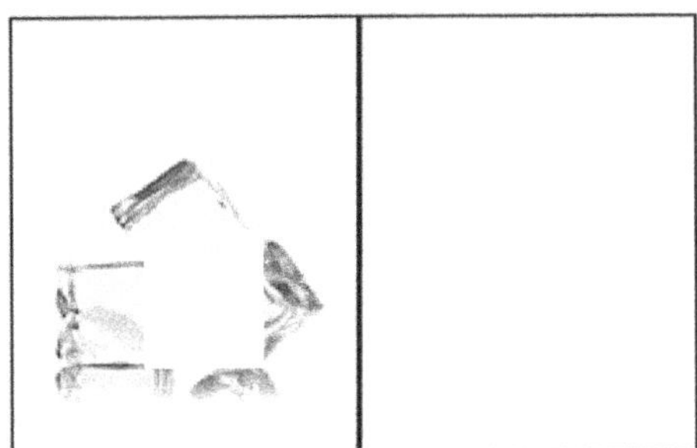

Paste the object with sound on the worksheet

WEEK 11: IDENTIFICATION OF SOUND "j"

Day 1

Reading of Sound "j"

Materials

- 3 Flash cards ("j" as Jug, Jaguar, Jet)
- Phonics bag.

Presentation

- Bring out the three flash cards.
- Place the cards on the table.
- Assemble the pupils together
- Read the sound and the object to the pupils and also ensure to show the body demonstration.
- Allow the pupils to pass the flash cards around.
- Return the flash cards to the phonics bag.
- Hang the bag back on the wall.

Day 2

Pasting of Sound "j" on Worksheet

Materials:

- My Phonics worksheet
- Pelican card of "j" sound
- Water gum
- Tray
- Towel

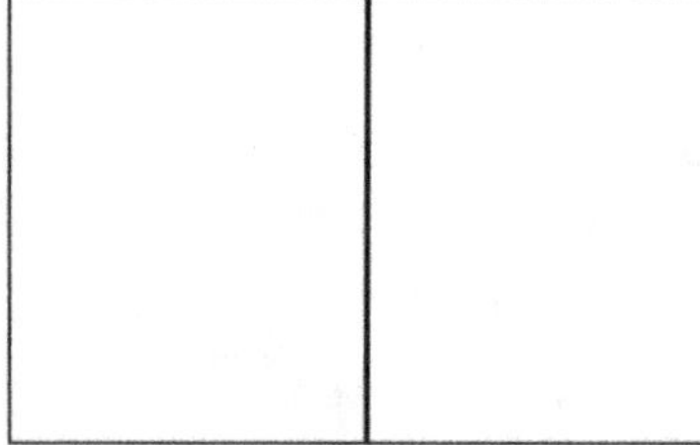

Presentation

- Bring out the required materials and place them on the table.
- Tell the pupils the name of the materials you have on the table.
- Call the pupils one by one to pick the "j" sound
- Provide them with a gum.
- Demonstrate to them how to wet the sound pelican card with gum
- Allow them all to wet the back of the sound with considerable amount of gum.
- Provide each pupil with their own Jolly phonics worksheet.
- Allow the pupils to paste the sound "j" on the provided worksheet.

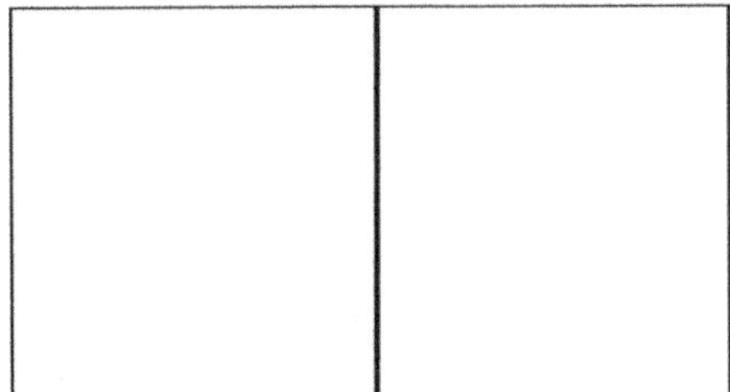

Paste the sound "j" Pelican card on the worksheet

Day 3

Pasting of Sound on Object

Materials

- Creative reading worksheets
- Gum
- Cutout object of jet
- cutout of sound "j"
- Tray

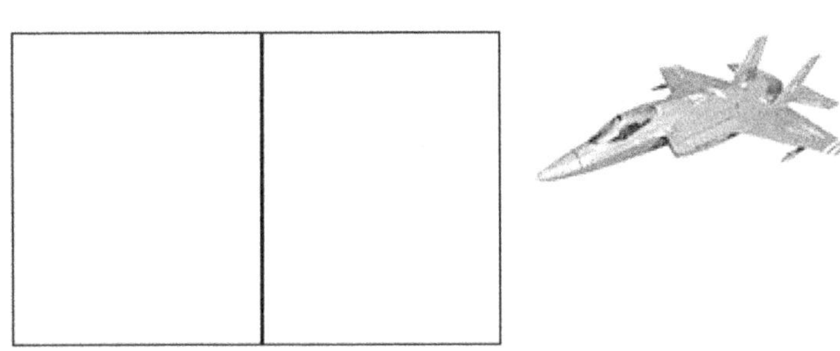

Presentation

- Bring out the required materials and place them on the table.
- Tell the pupils the name of the materials you have on the table.
- Call the pupils one by one to pick the "j" sound
- Demonstrate to them how to wet the sound pelican card with gum
- Allow them all to wet the back of the sound with considerable amount of gum and then paste it on the cutout object of jet.
- Bring out their worksheets and let them paste the object with sound on it.

Paste the cutout of sound "j" on the object jet

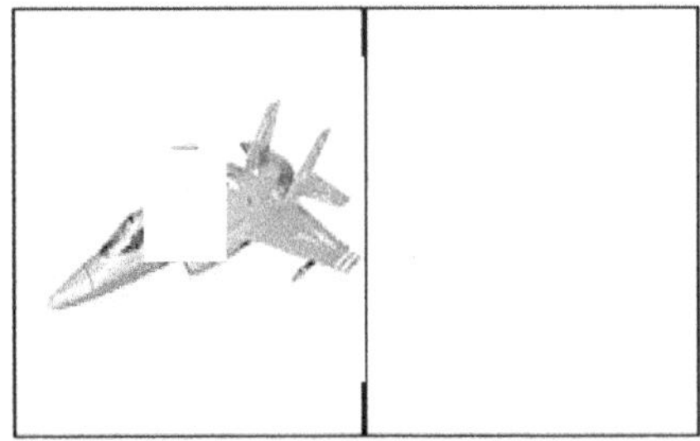

Paste the object jet with sound "j" on the worksheet

Day 4

Colouring of Sound with Object

Materials

- Exercise book
- Jumbo Crayon
- A stamp
- Object stamp
- Stamp pad

Presentation

- Bring out the required materials and place them on the table.
- Invite one child at a time to work with.
- Place the exercise book, crayon, and the stamp pad on the table for the child.
- Stamp the sound and the object on the exercise book.
- Ask the pupil to point at the objects
- Give the pupil the blue crayon to color the "j" sound.
- Give the pupil the yellow crayon to color the object.

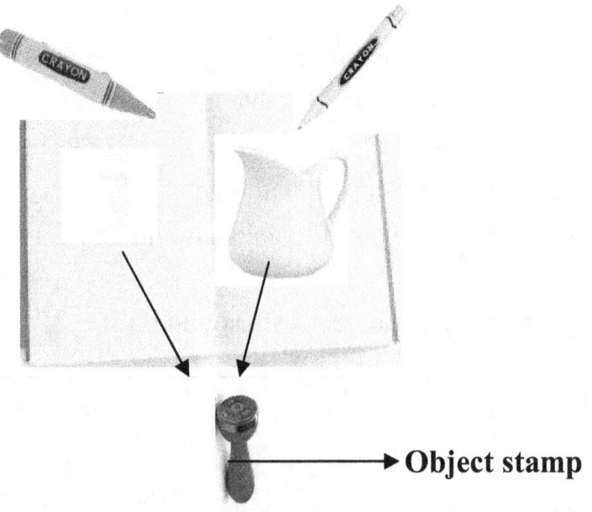

Colour the sound "j" in the exercise book with blue crayon

Colour the object jug in the exercise book with yellow crayon

Day 5

Pasting of Sound with Object "j" as Jaguar

Materials

- Creative reading worksheets
- Gum
- Cutout of sound with object "j" as in Jaguar.
- Tray

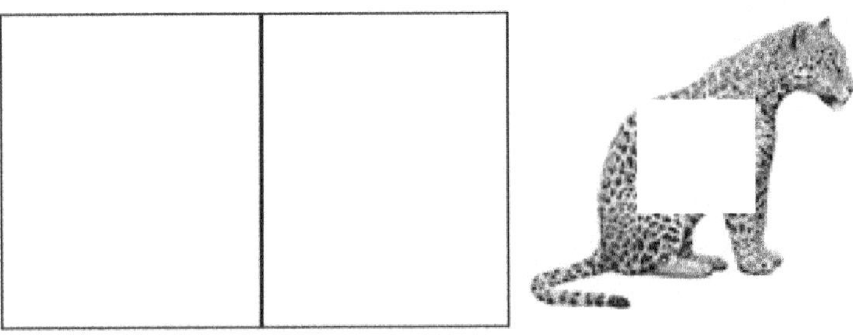

Presentation

- Bring out the required materials and place them on the table.
- Tell the pupils the name of the materials you have on the table.
- Call the pupils one by one to pick the cutout of sound with object "j" as in jaguar.
- Demonstrate to them how to wet the sound pelican card with gum.
- Allow them all to wet the back of the sound with object cutout with considerable amount of gum.
- Bring out their worksheets and let them paste the object with sound on it.

Paste the object with sound on the worksheet

WEEK 12: IDENTIFICATION OF SOUND "k"

Day 1

Reading of Sound "k"

Materials

- 3 Flash cards ("k" as key, kangaroo, King)
- Phonics bag.

Presentation

- Bring out the three flash cards.
- Place the cards on the table.
- Assemble the pupils together
- Read the sound and the object to the pupils and also ensure to show the body demonstration.
- Allow the pupils to pass the flash cards around.
- Return the flash cards to the phonics bag.
- Hang the bag back on the wall.

Day 2

Pasting of Sound "k" on Worksheet

Materials:

- My Phonics worksheet
- Pelican card of "k" sound
- Water gum
- Tray
- Towel

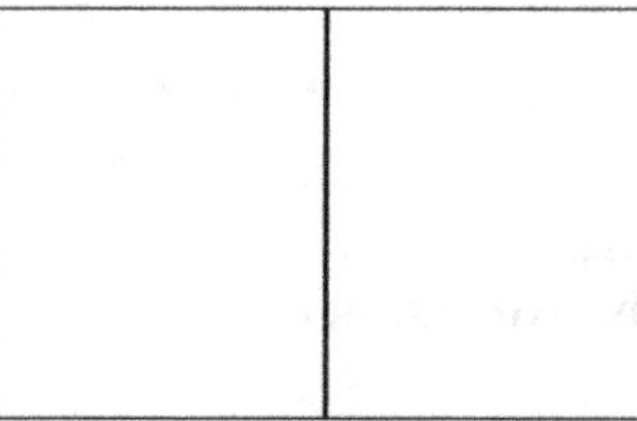

Presentation

- Bring out the required materials and place them on the table.
- Tell the pupils the name of the materials you have on the table.
- Call the pupils one by one to pick the "k" sound
- Provide them with a gum.
- Demonstrate to them how to wet the sound pelican card with gum

- Allow them all to wet the back of the sound with considerable amount of gum.
- Provide each pupil with their own Jolly phonics worksheet.
- Allow the pupils to paste the sound "k" on the provided worksheet.

Paste the sound "k" Pelican card on the worksheet

Day 3

Pasting of Sound on Object

Materials

- Creative reading worksheets
- Gum
- Cutout object of key
- cutout of sound "k"
- Tray

Presentation

- Bring out the required materials and place them on the table.
- Tell the pupils the name of the materials you have on the table.
- Call the pupils one by one to pick the "k" sound
- Demonstrate to them how to wet the sound pelican card with gum
- Allow them all to wet the back of the sound with considerable amount of gum and then paste it on the cutout object of key.
- Bring out their worksheets and let them paste the object with sound on it.

Paste the cutout of sound "k" on the object key

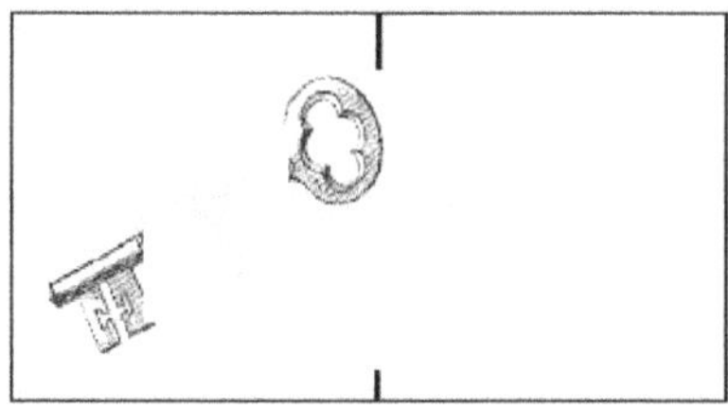

Paste the object key with sound "k" on the worksheet

Day 4

Colouring of Sound with Object

Materials

- Exercise book
- Jumbo Crayon
- A stamp
- Object stamp
- Stamp pad

Presentation

- Bring out the required materials and place them on the table.
- Invite one child at a time to work with.
- Place the exercise book, crayon, and the stamp pad on the table for the child.
- Stamp the sound and the object on the exercise book.
- Ask the pupil to point at the objects
- Give the pupil the blue crayon to color the "k" sound.
- Give the pupil the yellow crayon to color the object.

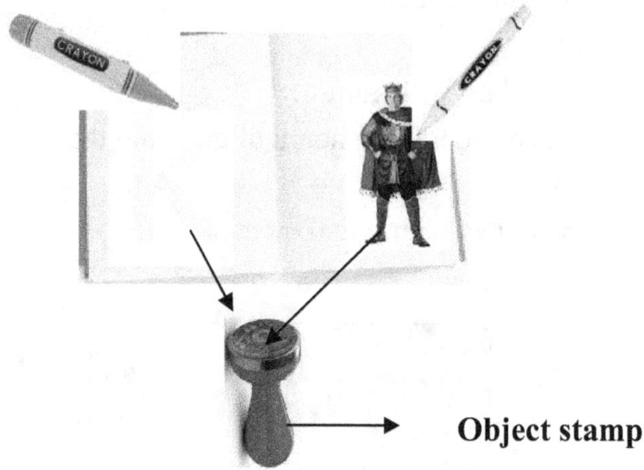

Object stamp

Colour the stamped sound "k" in the exercise book with blue crayon

Colour the stamped object king in the exercise book with yellow crayon

Day 5

Pasting of Sound with Object "k" as kangaroo

Materials

- Creative reading worksheets
- Gum
- Cutout of sound with object "k" as in kangaroo.

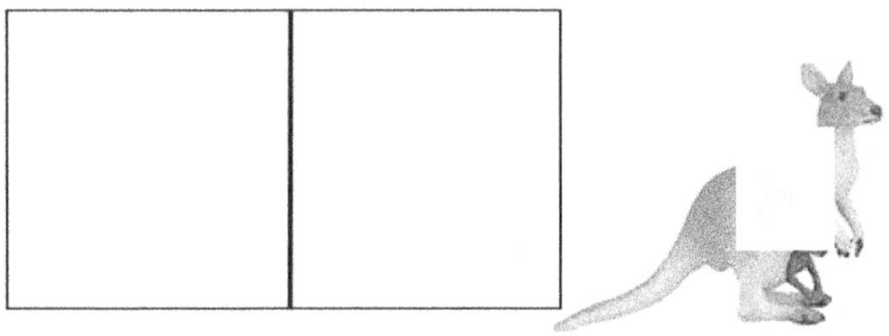

Presentation

- Bring out the required materials and place them on the table.
- Tell the pupils the name of the materials you have on the table.
- Call the pupils one by one to pick the cutout of sound with object "k" as in Kangaroo.
- Demonstrate to them how to wet the sound pelican card with gum.
- Allow them all to wet the back of the sound with object cutout with considerable amount of gum.
- Bring out their worksheets and let them paste the object with sound on it.

Paste the object with sound on the worksheet

Day 1

Reading of Sound "l"

Materials

- 3 Flash cards ("l" as Lamp, Leg, Lion)
- Phonics bag.

Presentation

- Bring out the three flash cards.
- Place the cards on the table.
- Assemble the pupils together
- Read the sound and the object to the pupils and also ensure to show the body demonstration.
- Allow the pupils to pass the flash cards around.
- Return the flash cards to the phonics bag.
- Hang the bag back on the wall.

Day 2

Pasting of Sound "l" on Worksheet

Materials:

- My Phonics worksheet
- Pelican card of "l" sound
- Water gum
- Tray
- Towel

Presentation

- Bring out the required materials and place them on the table.
- Tell the pupils the name of the materials you have on the table.
- Call the pupils one by one to pick the "l" sound
- Provide them with a gum.
- Demonstrate to them how to wet the sound pelican card with gum
- Allow them all to wet the back of the sound with considerable amount of gum.
- Provide each pupil with their own Jolly phonics worksheet.
- Allow the pupils to paste the sound "l" on the provided worksheet.

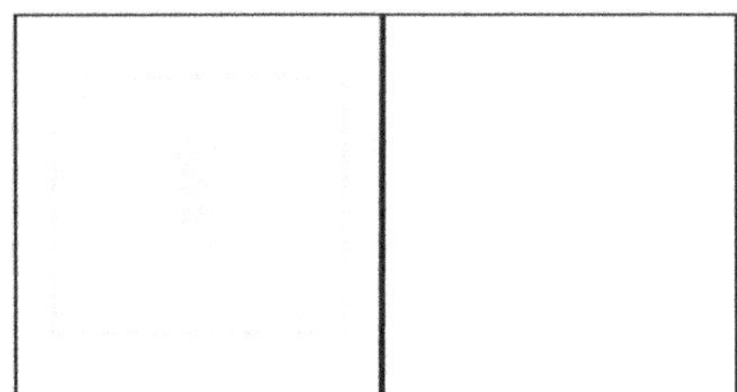

Paste the sound "l" Pelican card on the worksheet

Day 3

Pasting of Sound on Object

Materials

- Creative reading worksheets
- Gum
- Cutout object of lamp
- cutout of sound "l"
- Tray

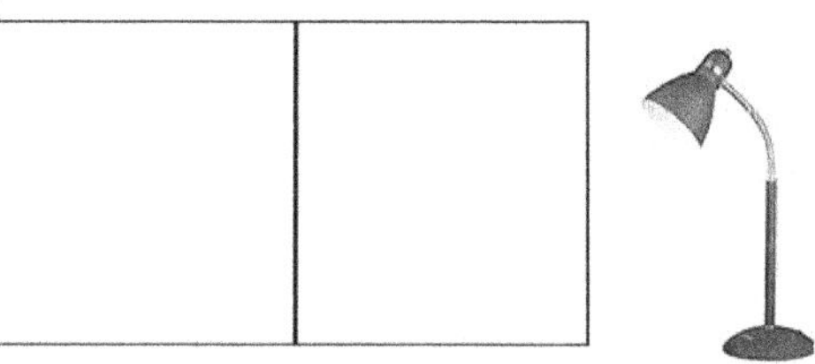

Presentation

- Bring out the required materials and place them on the table.
- Tell the pupils the name of the materials you have on the table.
- Call the pupils one by one to pick the "l" sound
- Demonstrate to them how to wet the sound pelican card with gum
- Allow them all to wet the back of the sound with considerable amount of gum and then paste it on the cutout object of lamp.
- Bring out their worksheets and let them paste the object with sound on it.

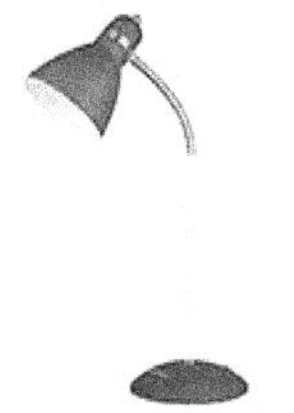

Paste the cutout of sound "l" on the object lamp

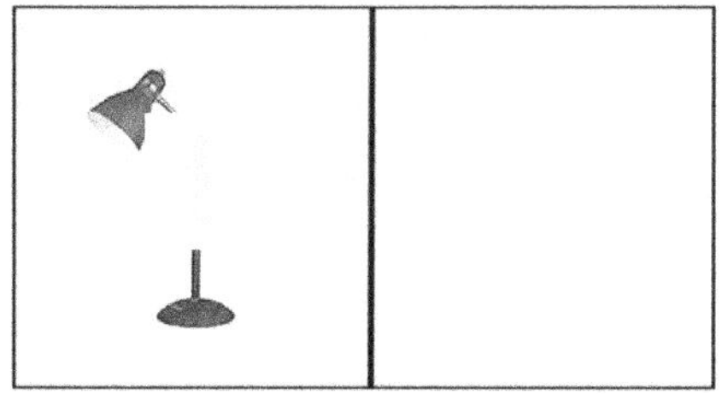

Paste the object lamp with sound "l" on the worksheet

Day 4

Colouring of Sound with Object

Materials

- Exercise book
- Jumbo Crayon
- A stamp
- Object stamp
- Stamp pad

Presentation

- Bring out the required materials and place them on the table.
- Invite one child at a time to work with.
- Place the exercise book, crayon, and the stamp pad on the table for the child.
- Stamp the sound and the object on the exercise book.
- Ask the pupil to point at the objects
- Give the pupil the blue crayon to color the "l" sound.
- Give the pupil the yellow crayon to color the object.

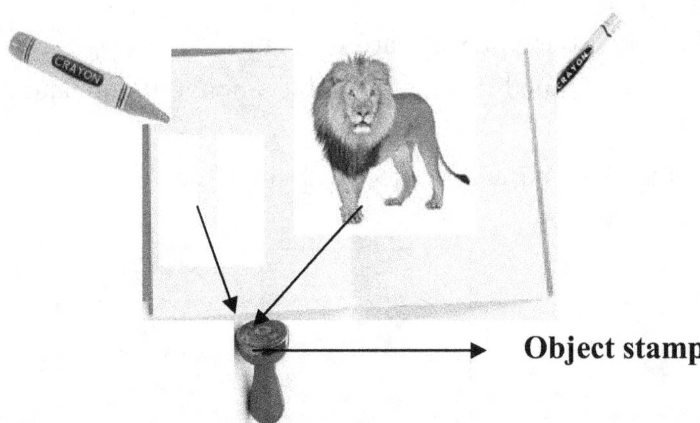

Colour the stamped sound "l" in the exercise book with blue crayon

Colour the stamped object lion in the exercise book with yellow crayon

Day 5

Pasting of Sound with Object "l" as Leg

Materials

- Creative reading worksheets
- Gum
- Cutout of sound with object "l" as in leg.

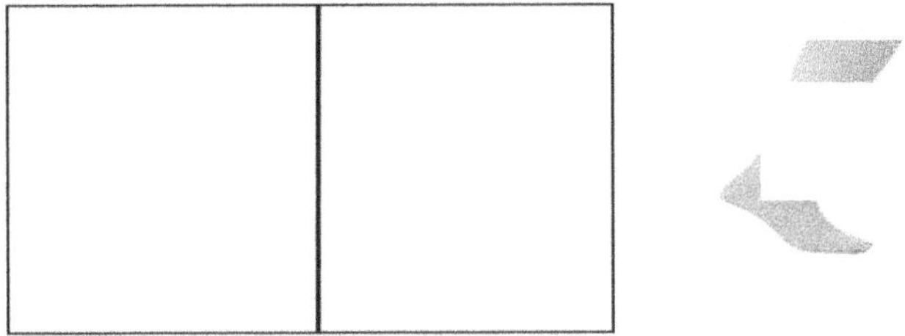

Presentation

- Bring out the required materials and place them on the table.
- Tell the pupils the name of the materials you have on the table.
- Call the pupils one by one to pick the cutout of sound with object "l" as in leg.
- Demonstrate to them how to wet the sound pelican card with gum.
- Allow them all to wet the back of the sound with object cutout with considerable amount of gum.
- Bring out their worksheets and let them paste the object with sound on it.

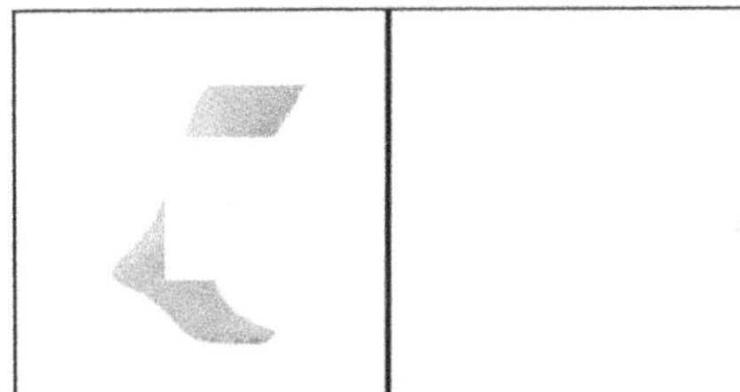

Paste the object with sound on the worksheet

<h1 align="center">WEEK 14: IDENTIFICATION OF SOUND "m"</h1>

Day 1

Reading of Sound "m"

Materials

- 3 Flash cards ("m" as Man, mat, mice)
- Phonics bag.

Presentation

- Bring out the three flash cards.
- Place the cards on the table.
- Assemble the pupils together
- Read the sound and the object to the pupils and also ensure to show the body demonstration.
- Allow the pupils to pass the flash cards around.
- Return the flash cards to the phonics bag.
- Hang the bag back on the wall.

Day 2

Pasting of Sound "m" on Worksheet

Materials:

- My Phonics worksheet
- Pelican card of "m" sound
- Water gum
- Tray
- Towel

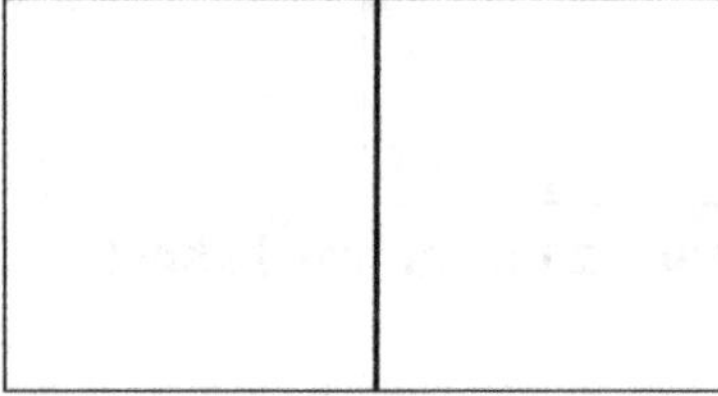

Presentation

- Bring out the required materials and place them on the table.
- Tell the pupils the name of the materials you have on the table.
- Call the pupils one by one to pick the "m" sound
- Provide them with a gum.
- Demonstrate to them how to wet the sound pelican card with gum
- Allow them all to wet the back of the sound with considerable amount of gum.
- Provide each pupil with their own Jolly phonics worksheet.
- Allow the pupils to paste the sound "m" on the provided worksheet.

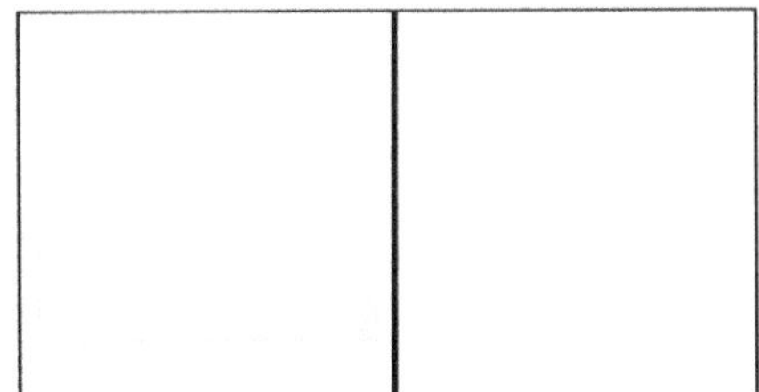

Paste the sound "m" Pelican card on the worksheet

Day 3

Pasting of Sound on Object

Materials

- Creative reading worksheets
- Gum
- Cutout object of mice
- cutout of sound "m"
- Tray

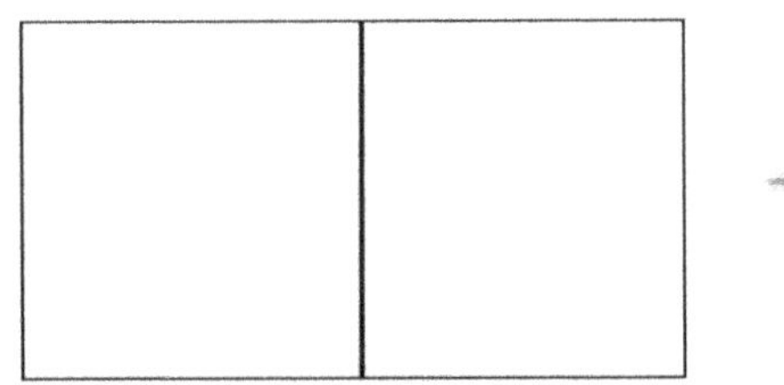

Presentation

- Bring out the required materials and place them on the table.
- Tell the pupils the name of the materials you have on the table.
- Call the pupils one by one to pick the "m" sound
- Demonstrate to them how to wet the sound pelican card with gum
- Allow them all to wet the back of the sound with considerable amount of gum and then paste it on the cutout object of mice.
- Bring out their worksheets and let them paste the object with sound on it.

Paste the cutout of sound "m" on the object mice

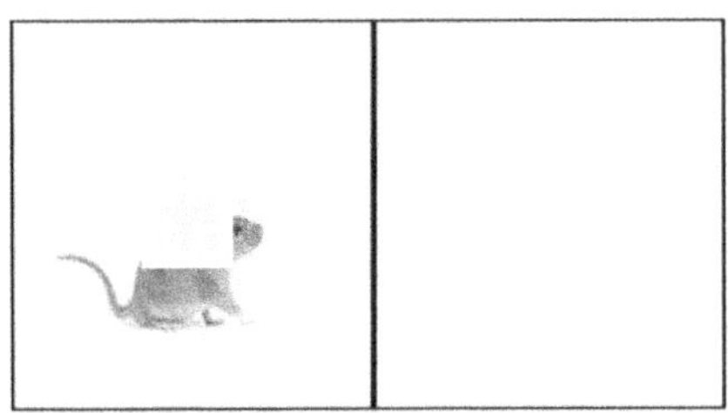

Paste the object mice with sound "m" on the worksheet

Day 4

Colouring of Sound with Object

Materials

- Exercise book
- Jumbo Crayon
- A stamp
- Object stamp
- Stamp pad

Presentation

- Bring out the required materials and place them on the table.
- Invite one child at a time to work with.
- Place the exercise book, crayon, and the stamp pad on the table for the child.
- Stamp the sound and the object on the exercise book.
- Ask the pupil to point at the objects
- Give the pupil the blue crayon to color the "m" sound.
- Give the pupil the yellow crayon to color the object.

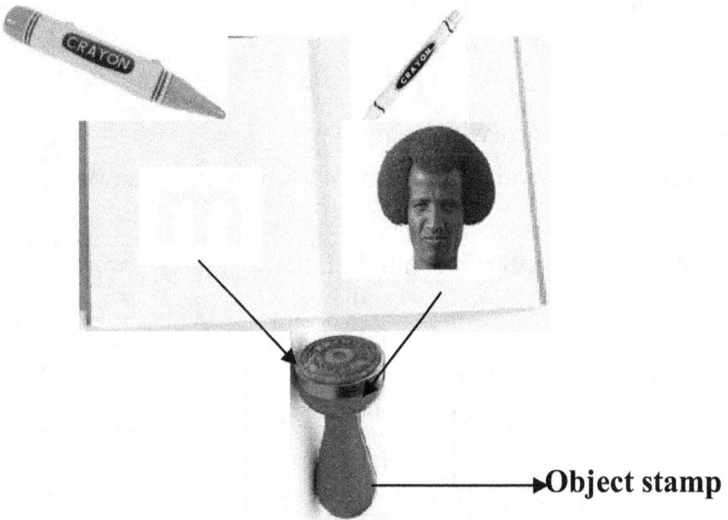

Colour the stamped sound "m" in the exercise book with blue crayon

Colour the stamped object man in the exercise book with yellow crayon

Day 5

Pasting of Sound with Object "m" as mat

Materials

- Creative reading worksheets
- Gum
- Cutout of sound with object "m" as in mat.

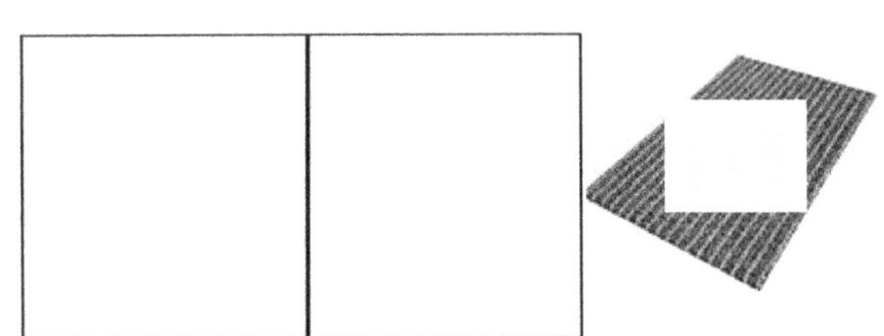

Presentation

- Bring out the required materials and place them on the table.
- Tell the pupils the name of the materials you have on the table.
- Call the pupils one by one to pick the cutout of sound with object "m" as in mat.
- Demonstrate to them how to wet the sound pelican card with gum.
- Allow them all to wet the back of the sound with object cutout with considerable amount of gum.
- Bring out their worksheets and let them paste the object with sound on it.

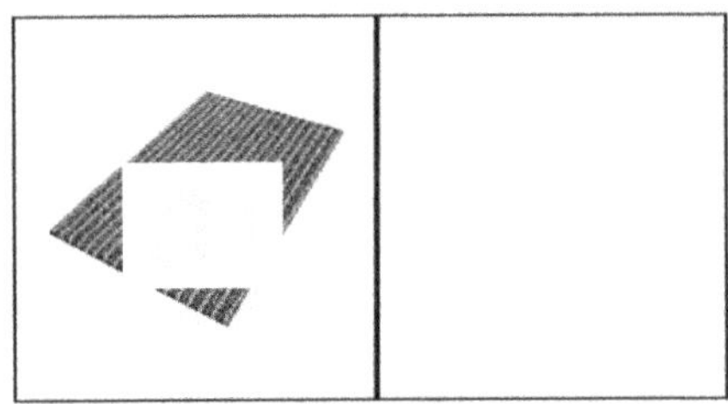

Paste the object with sound on the worksheet

WEEK 15: IDENTIFICATION OF SOUND "n"

Day 1

Reading of Sound "n"

Materials

- 3 Flash cards ("n" as Nurse, Nose, Needle)
- Phonics bag.

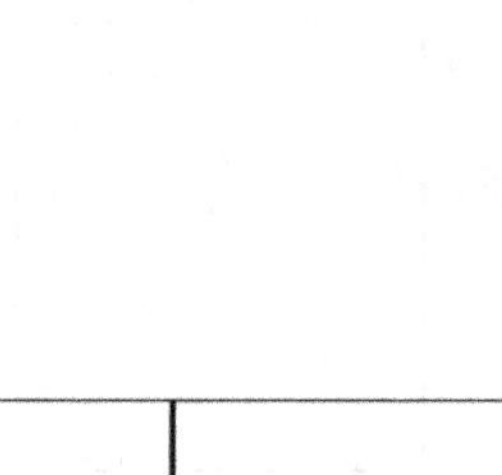

Presentation

- Bring out the three flash cards.
- Place the cards on the table.
- Assemble the pupils together
- Read the sound and the object to the pupils and also ensure to show the body demonstration.
- Allow the pupils to pass the flash cards around.
- Return the flash cards to the phonics bag.
- Hang the bag back on the wall.

Day 2

Pasting of Sound "n" on Worksheet

Materials:

- My Phonics worksheet
- Pelican card of "n" sound
- Water gum
- Tray
- Towel

Presentation

- Bring out the required materials and place them on the table.
- Tell the pupils the name of the materials you have on the table.
- Call the pupils one by one to pick the "n" sound
- Provide them with a gum.
- Demonstrate to them how to wet the sound pelican card with gum
- Allow them all to wet the back of the sound with considerable amount of gum.
- Provide each pupil with their own Jolly phonics worksheet.
- Allow the pupils to paste the sound "n" on the provided worksheet.

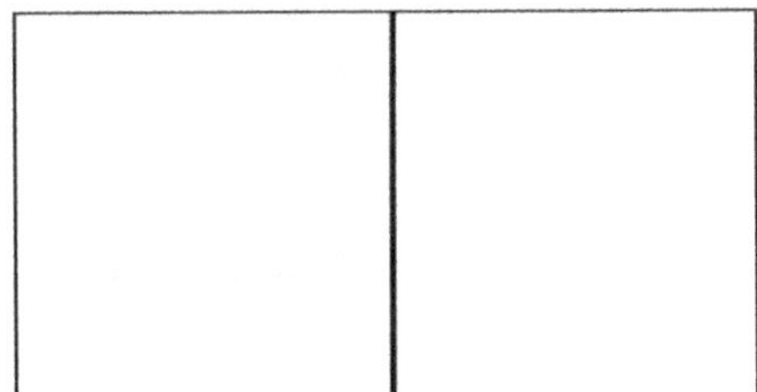

Paste the sound "n" Pelican card on the worksheet

Day 3

Pasting of Sound on Object

Materials

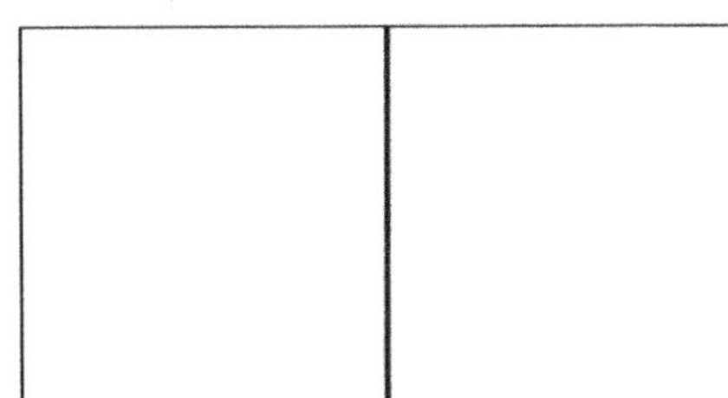
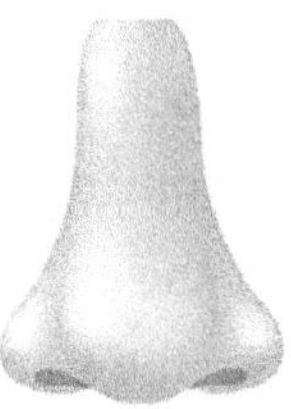

- Creative reading worksheets
- Gum
- Cutout object of nose
- cutout of sound "n"
- Tray

Presentation

- Bring out the required materials and place them on the table.
- Tell the pupils the name of the materials you have on the table.
- Call the pupils one by one to pick the "n" sound
- Demonstrate to them how to wet the sound pelican card with gum
- Allow them all to wet the back of the sound with considerable amount of gum and then paste it on the cutout object of nose.
- Bring out their worksheets and let them paste the object with sound on it.

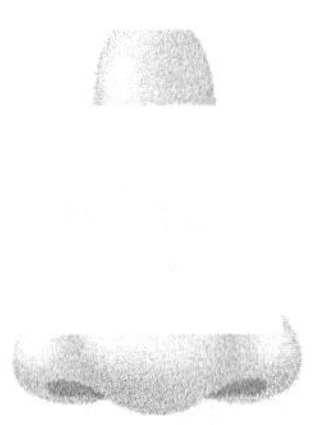

Paste the cutout of sound "n" on the object nose

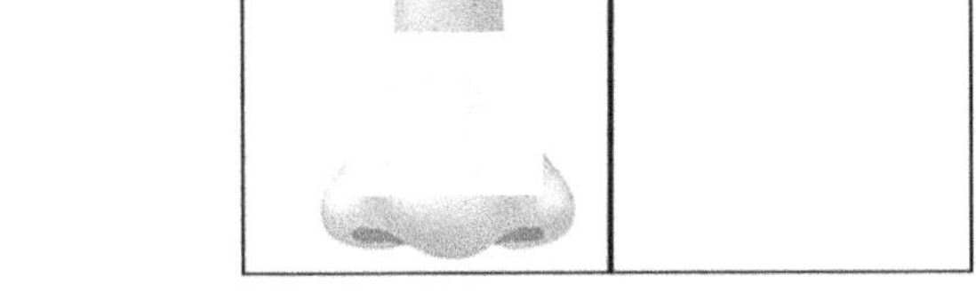

Paste the object nose with sound "n" on the worksheet

Day 4- Colouring of Sound with Object

Materials

- Exercise book
- Jumbo Crayon
- A stamp
- Object stamp
- Stamp pad

Presentation

- Bring out the required materials and place them on the table.
- Invite one child at a time to work with.
- Place the exercise book, crayon, and the stamp pad on the table for the child.
- Stamp the sound and the object on the exercise book.
- Ask the pupil to point at the objects
- Give the pupil the blue crayon to color the "n" sound.
- Give the pupil the yellow crayon to color the object.

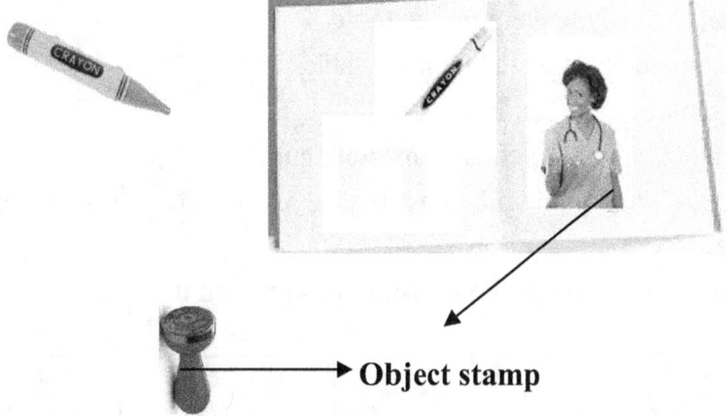

Colour the stamped sound "n" in the exercise book with blue crayon

Colour the stamped object nurse in the exercise book with yellow crayon

Day 5

Pasting of Sound with Object "n" as in Needle

Materials

- Creative reading worksheets
- Gum
- Cutout of sound with object "n" as in needle.

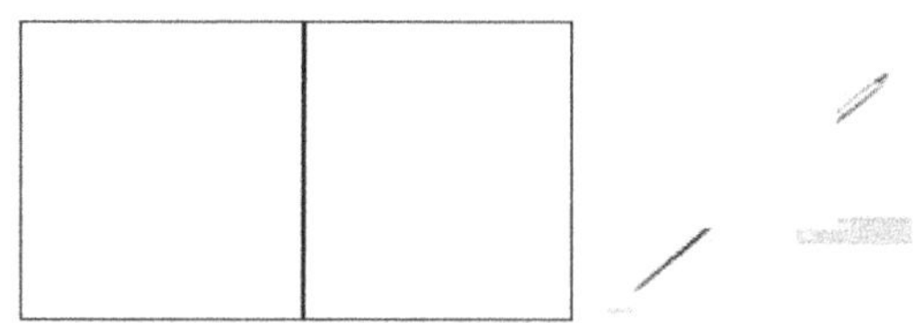

Presentation

- Bring out the required materials and place them on the table.
- Tell the pupils the name of the materials you have on the table.
- Call the pupils one by one to pick the cutout of sound with object "n" as in Needle.
- Demonstrate to them how to wet the sound pelican card with gum.
- Allow them all to wet the back of the sound with object cutout with considerable amount of gum.
- Bring out their worksheets and let them paste the object with sound on it.

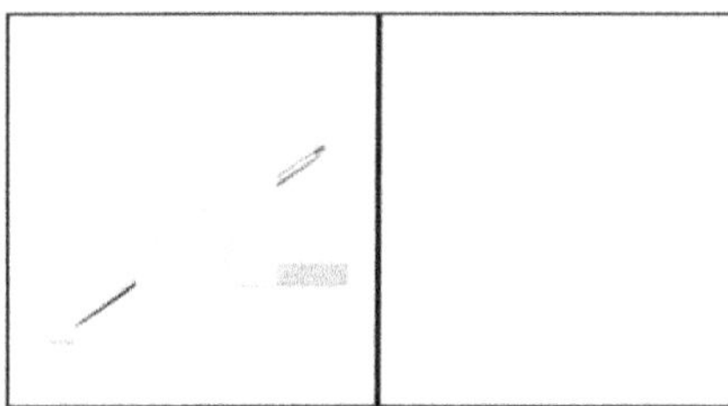

Paste the object with sound on the worksheet

Day 1

Reading of Sound "o"

Materials

- 3 Flash cards ("o" as Onion, Octopus, Okra)
- Phonics bag.

Presentation

- Bring out the three flash cards.
- Place the cards on the table.
- Assemble the pupils together
- Read the sound and the object to the pupils and also ensure to show the body demonstration.
- Allow the pupils to pass the flash cards around.
- Return the flash cards to the phonics bag.
- Hang the bag back on the wall.

Day 2

Pasting of Sound "o" on Worksheet

Materials:

- My Phonics worksheet
- Pelican card of "o" sound
- Water gum
- Tray
- Towel

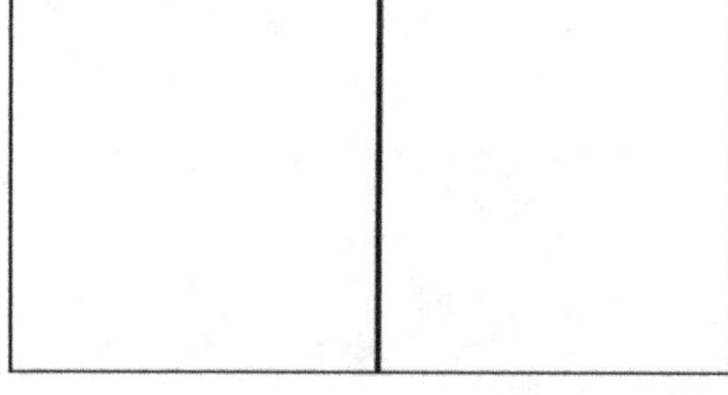

Presentation

- Bring out the required materials and place them on the table.
- Tell the pupils the name of the materials you have on the table.
- Call the pupils one by one to pick the "o" sound
- Provide them with a gum.
- Demonstrate to them how to wet the sound pelican card with gum
- Allow them all to wet the back of the sound with considerable amount of gum.
- Provide each pupil with their own Jolly phonics worksheet.
- Allow the pupils to paste the sound "o" on the provided worksheet.

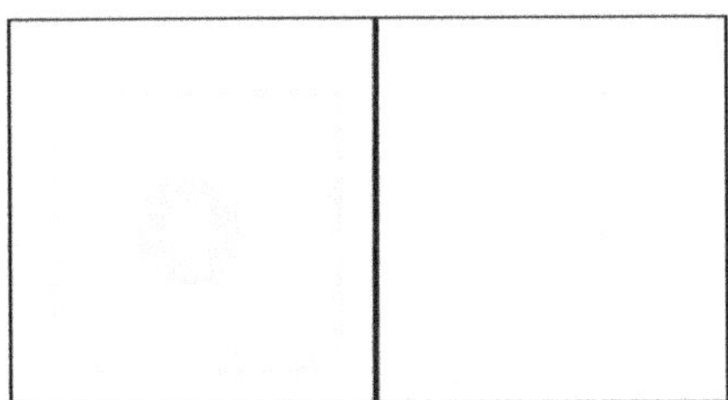

Paste the sound "o" Pelican card on the worksheet

Day 3

Pasting of Sound on Object

Materials

- Creative reading worksheets
- Gum
- Cutout object of ball
- cutout of sound "o"
- Tray

Presentation

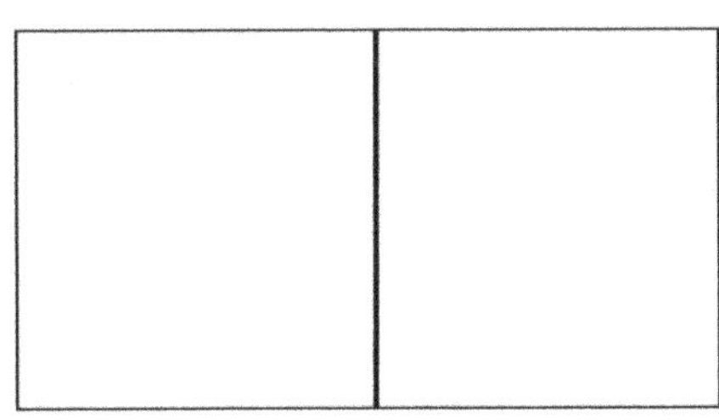

- Bring out the required materials and place them on the table.
- Tell the pupils the name of the materials you have on the table.
- Call the pupils one by one to pick the "o" sound
- Demonstrate to them how to wet the sound pelican card with gum
- Allow them all to wet the back of the sound with considerable amount of gum and then paste it on the cutout object of onion.
- Bring out their worksheets and let them paste the object with sound on it.

Paste the cutout of sound "o" on the object onion

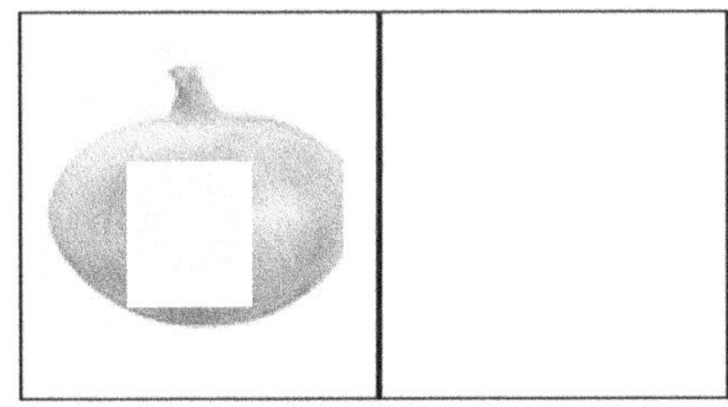

Paste the object onion with sound "o" on the worksheet

Day 4

Colouring of Sound with Object

Materials

- Exercise book
- Jumbo Crayon
- A stamp
- Object stamp

- Stamp pad

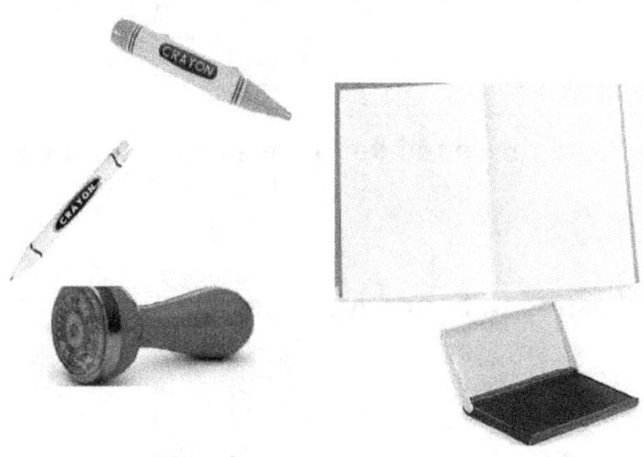

Presentation

- Bring out the required materials and place them on the table.
- Invite one child at a time to work with.
- Place the exercise book, crayon, and the stamp pad on the table for the child.
- Stamp the sound and the object on the exercise book.
- Ask the pupil to point at the objects
- Give the pupil the blue crayon to color the "o" sound.
- Give the pupil the yellow crayon to color the object.

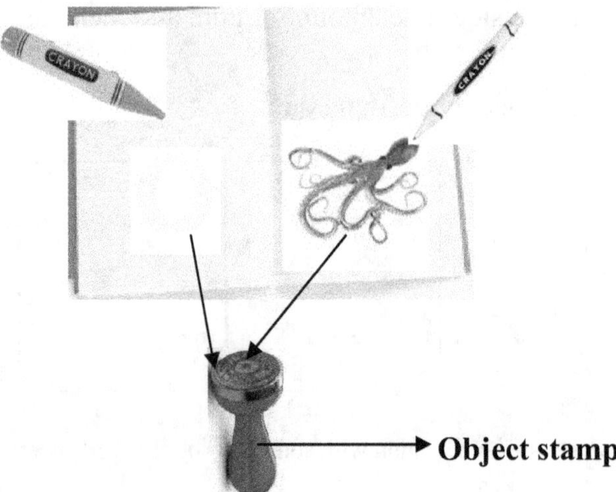

Colour the stamped sound "o" in the exercise book with blue crayon

Colour the stamped object octopus in the exercise book with yellow crayon

Day 5

Pasting of Sound with Object "o" as okra

Materials

- Creative reading worksheets
- Gum
- Cutout of sound with object "o" as in okra.

Presentation

- Bring out the required materials and place them on the table.
- Tell the pupils the name of the materials you have on the table.
- Call the pupils one by one to pick the cutout of sound with object "o" as in okra.
- Demonstrate to them how to wet the sound pelican card with gum.
- Allow them all to wet the back of the sound with object cutout with considerable amount of gum.
- Bring out their worksheets and let them paste the object with sound on it.

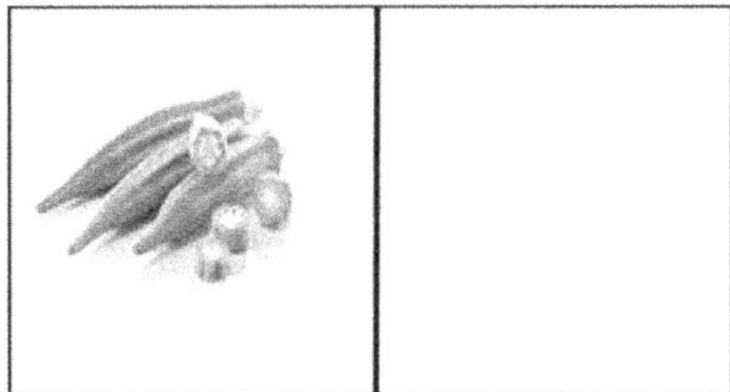

Paste the object with sound on the worksheet

<h1 style="text-align:center">WEEK 15: IDENTIFICATION OF SOUND "p"</h1>

Day 1

Reading of Sound "p"

Materials

- 3 Flash cards ("p" as Pen, Pot, Penguin)
- Phonics bag.

Presentation

- Bring out the three flash cards.
- Place the cards on the table.
- Assemble the pupils together
- Read the sound and the object to the pupils and also ensure to show the body demonstration.
- Allow the pupils to pass the flash cards around.
- Return the flash cards to the phonics bag.
- Hang the bag back on the wall.

Day 2

Pasting of Sound "p" on Worksheet

Materials:

- My Phonics worksheet
- Pelican card of "p" sound
- Water gum
- Tray
- Towel

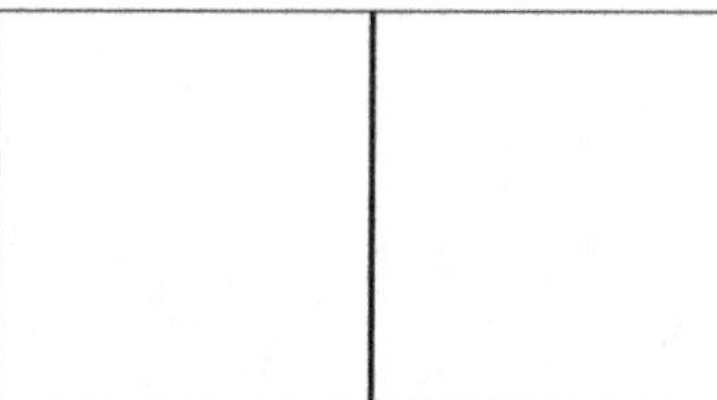

Presentation

- Bring out the required materials and place them on the table.
- Tell the pupils the name of the materials you have on the table.
- Call the pupils one by one to pick the "p" sound
- Provide them with a gum.
- Demonstrate to them how to wet the sound pelican card with gum
- Allow them all to wet the back of the sound with considerable amount of gum.
- Provide each pupil with their own Jolly phonics worksheet.
- Allow the pupils to paste the sound "p" on the provided worksheet.

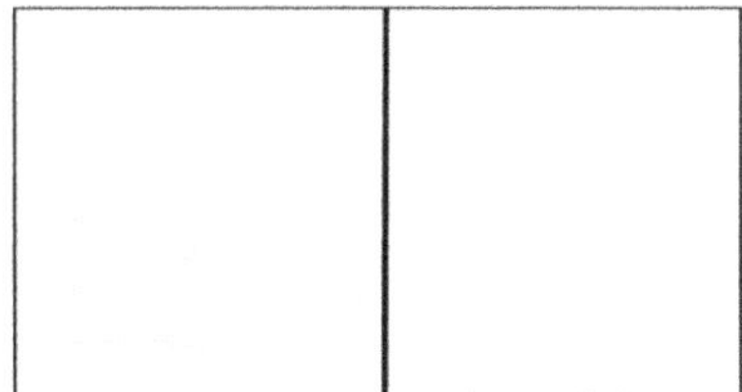

Paste the sound "p" Pelican card on the worksheet

Day 3

Pasting of Sound on Object

Materials

- Creative reading worksheets
- Gum
- Cutout object of pot
- cutout of sound "p"
- Tray

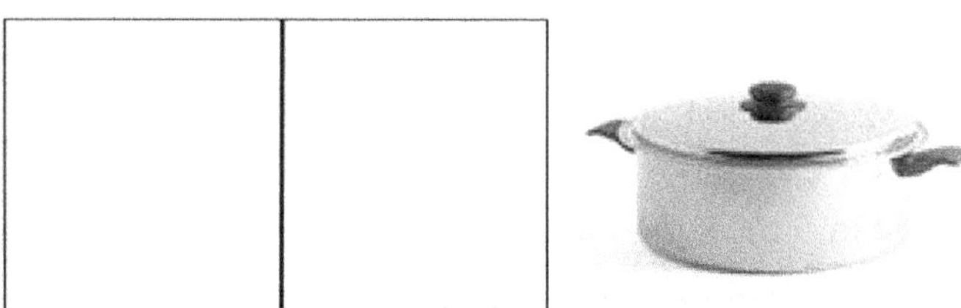

Presentation

- Bring out the required materials and place them on the table.
- Tell the pupils the name of the materials you have on the table.
- Call the pupils one by one to pick the "p" sound
- Demonstrate to them how to wet the sound pelican card with gum
- Allow them all to wet the back of the sound with considerable amount of gum and then paste it on the cutout object of pot.
- Bring out their worksheets and let them paste the object with sound on it.

Paste the cutout of sound "p" on the object pot

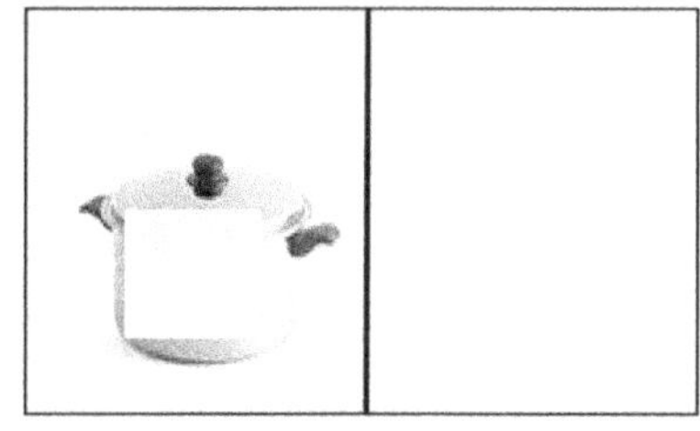

Paste the object pot with sound "p" on the worksheet

Day 4

Colouring of Sound with Object

Materials

- Exercise book
- Jumbo Crayon
- A stamp
- Object stamp
- Stamp pad

Presentation

- Bring out the required materials and place them on the table.
- Invite one child at a time to work with.
- Place the exercise book, crayon, and the stamp pad on the table for the child.
- Stamp the sound and the object on the exercise book.
- Ask the pupil to point at the objects
- Give the pupil the blue crayon to color the "p" sound.
- Give the pupil the yellow crayon to color the object.

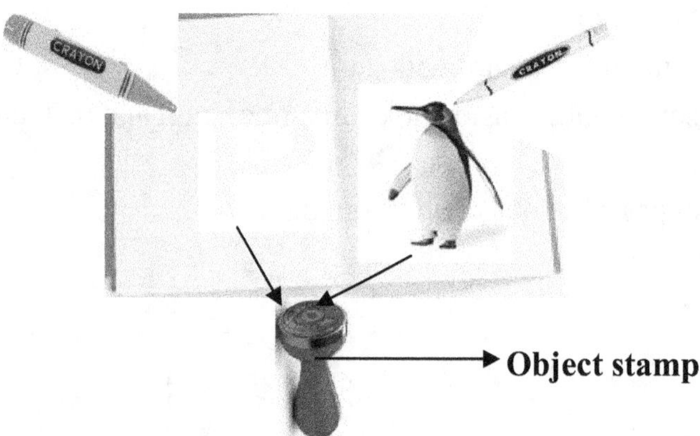

Colour the stamped sound "p" in the exercise book with blue crayon

Colour the stamped object penguin in the exercise book with yellow crayon

Day 5

Pasting of Sound with Object "p" as Pen

Materials

- Creative reading worksheets
- Gum
- Cutout of sound with object "p" as in penguin.

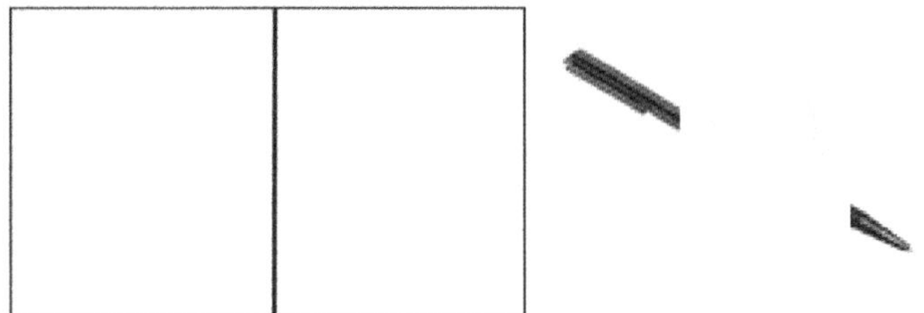

Presentation

- Bring out the required materials and place them on the table.
- Tell the pupils the name of the materials you have on the table.
- Call the pupils one by one to pick the cutout of sound with object "p" as in pen.
- Demonstrate to them how to wet the sound pelican card with gum.
- Allow them all to wet the back of the sound with object cutout with considerable amount of gum.
- Bring out their worksheets and let them paste the object with sound on it.

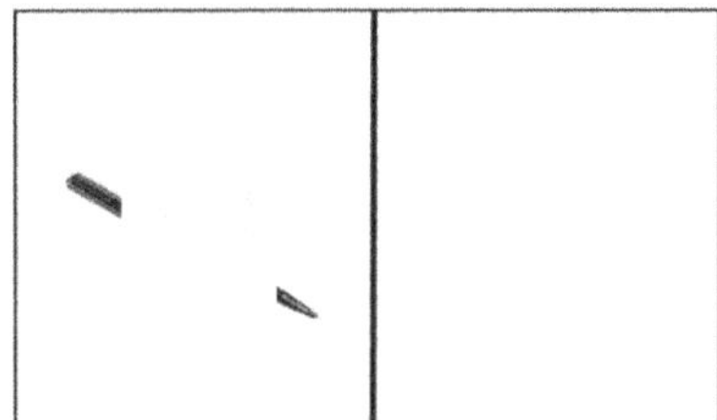

Paste the object with sound on the worksheet

Day 1

Reading of Sound "q"

Materials

- 3 Flash cards ("q" as Quill, Queen, Quail)
- Phonics bag.

Presentation

- Bring out the three flash cards.
- Place the cards on the table.
- Assemble the pupils together
- Read the sound and the object to the pupils and also ensure to show the body demonstration.
- Allow the pupils to pass the flash cards around.
- Return the flash cards to the phonics bag.
- Hang the bag back on the wall.

Day 2

Pasting of Sound "q" on Worksheet

Materials:

- My Phonics worksheet
- Pelican card of "q" sound
- Water gum
- Tray
- Towel

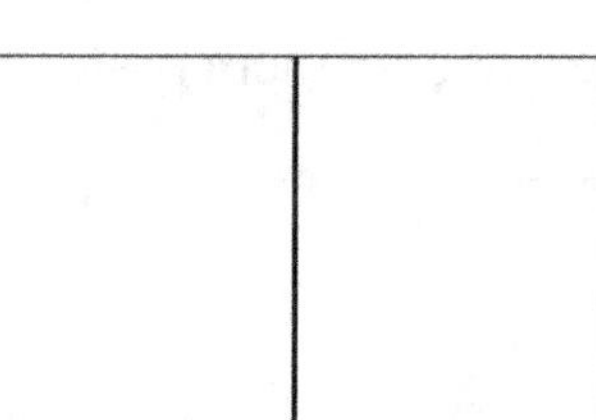

Presentation

- Bring out the required materials and place them on the table.
- Tell the pupils the name of the materials you have on the table.
- Call the pupils one by one to pick the "q" sound
- Provide them with a gum.
- Demonstrate to them how to wet the sound pelican card with gum
- Allow them all to wet the back of the sound with considerable amount of gum.
- Provide each pupil with their own Jolly phonics worksheet.
- Allow the pupils to paste the sound "q" on the provided worksheet.

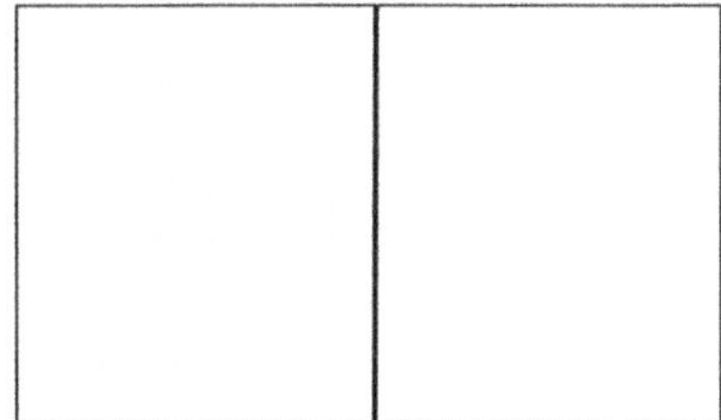

Paste the sound "q" Pelican card on the worksheet

Day 3

Pasting of Sound on Object

Materials

- Creative reading worksheets
- Gum
- Cutout object of a queen
- cutout of sound "q"
- Tray

Presentation

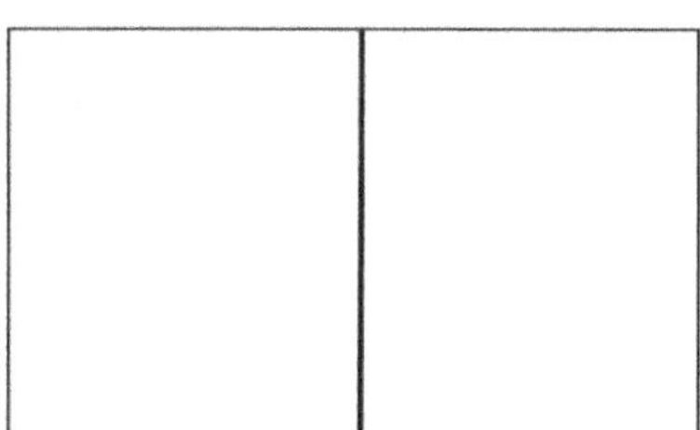

- Bring out the required materials and place them on the table.
- Tell the pupils the name of the materials you have on the table.
- Call the pupils one by one to pick the "q" sound
- Demonstrate to them how to wet the sound pelican card with gum
- Allow them all to wet the back of the sound with considerable amount of gum and then paste it on the cutout object of queen.
- Bring out their worksheets and let them paste the object with sound on it.

Paste the cutout of sound "q" on the object queen

Paste the object queen with sound "q" on the worksheet

Day 4

Colouring of Sound with Object

Materials

- Exercise book
- Jumbo Crayon
- A stamp
- Object stamp
- Stamp pad

Presentation

- Bring out the required materials and place them on the table.
- Invite one child at a time to work with.
- Place the exercise book, crayon, and the stamp pad on the table for the child.
- Stamp the sound and the object on the exercise book.
- Ask the pupil to point at the objects
- Give the pupil the blue crayon to color the "q" sound.
- Give the pupil the yellow crayon to color the object.

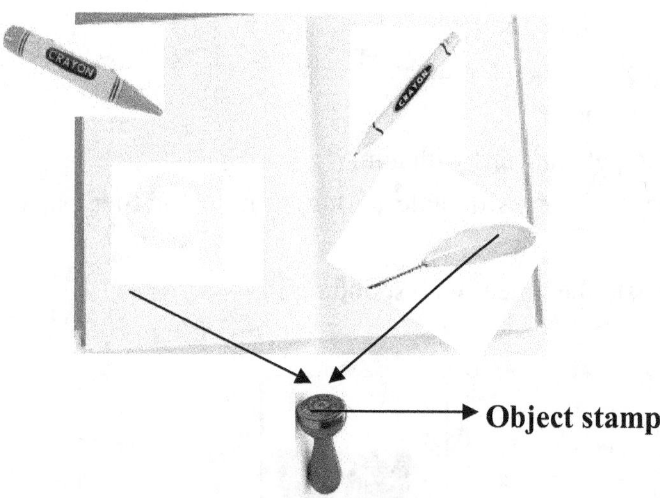

Colour the stamped sound "q" in the exercise book with blue crayon

Colour the stamped object quill in the exercise book with yellow crayon

Day 5

Pasting of Sound with Object "q" as in Quail.

Materials

- Creative reading worksheets
- Gum
- Cutout of sound with object "q" as in quail.

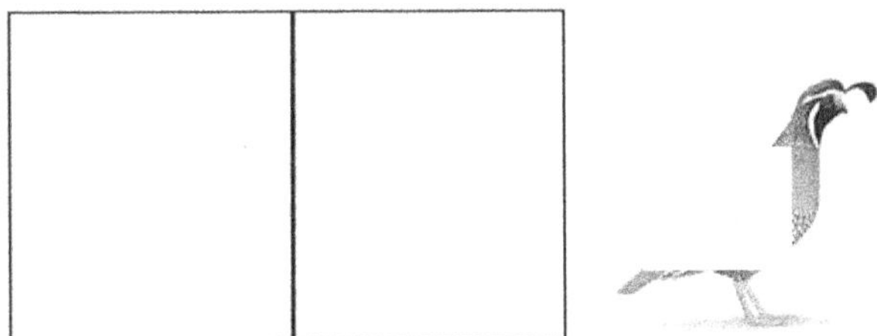

Presentation

- Bring out the required materials and place them on the table.
- Tell the pupils the name of the materials you have on the table.
- Call the pupils one by one to pick the cutout of sound with object "q" as in quail.
- Demonstrate to them how to wet the sound pelican card with gum.
- Allow them all to wet the back of the sound with object cutout with considerable amount of gum.
- Bring out their worksheets and let them paste the object with sound on it.

Paste the object with sound on the worksheet

Day 1

Reading of Sound "r"

Materials

- 3 Flash cards ("r" as Rabbit, Ram, Ruler)
- Phonics bag.

Presentation

- Bring out the three flash cards.
- Place the cards on the table.
- Assemble the pupils together
- Read the sound and the object to the pupils and also ensure to show the body demonstration.
- Allow the pupils to pass the flash cards around.
- Return the flash cards to the phonics bag.
- Hang the bag back on the wall.

Day 2

Pasting of Sound "r" on Worksheet

Materials:

- My Phonics worksheet
- Pelican card of "r" sound
- Water gum
- Tray
- Towel

Presentation

- Bring out the required materials and place them on the table.
- Tell the pupils the name of the materials you have on the table.
- Call the pupils one by one to pick the "r" sound
- Provide them with a gum.
- Demonstrate to them how to wet the sound pelican card with gum
- Allow them all to wet the back of the sound with considerable amount of gum.
- Provide each pupil with their own Jolly phonics worksheet.
- Allow the pupils to paste the sound "r" on the provided worksheet.

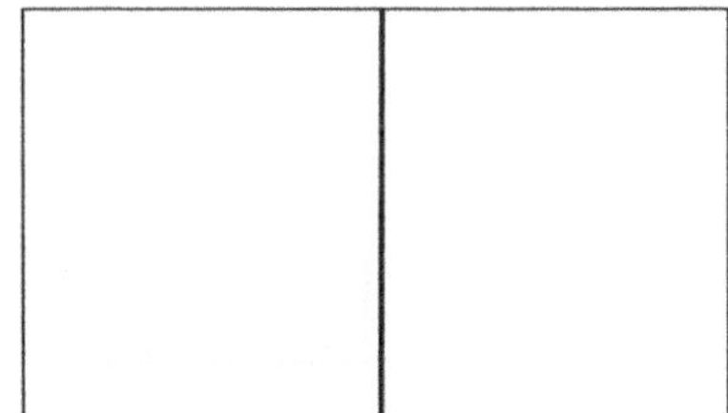

Paste the sound "r" Pelican card on the worksheet

Day 3

Pasting of Sound on Object

Materials

- Creative reading worksheets
- Gum
- Cutout object of ruler
- cutout of sound "r"
- Tray

Presentation

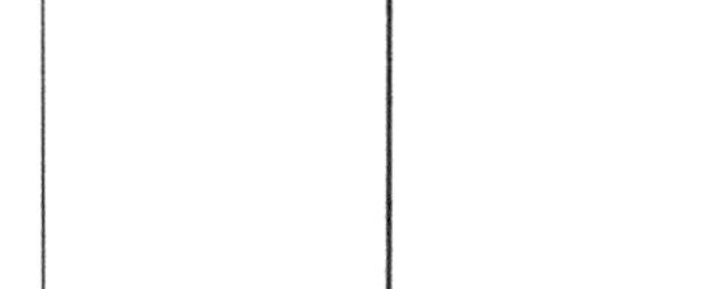

- Bring out the required materials and place them on the table.
- Tell the pupils the name of the materials you have on the table.
- Call the pupils one by one to pick the "r" sound
- Demonstrate to them how to wet the sound pelican card with gum
- Allow them all to wet the back of the sound with considerable amount of gum and then paste it on the cutout object of ram.
- Bring out their worksheets and let them paste the object with sound on it.

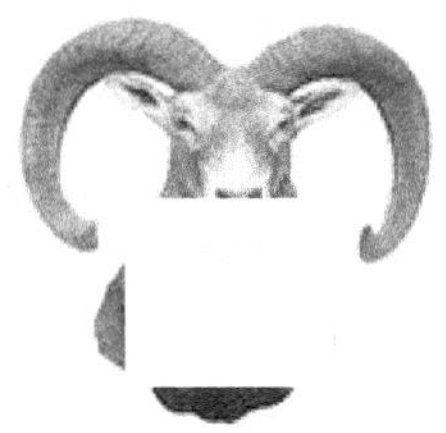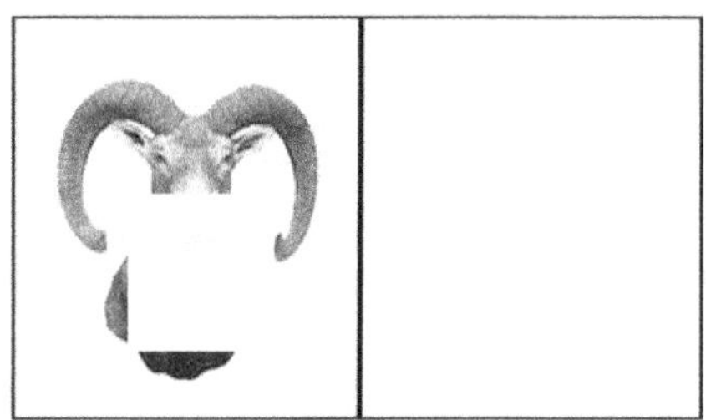

Paste the cutout of sound "r" on the object ram   Paste the object ram with sound "r" on the worksheet

Day 4

Colouring of Sound with Object

Materials

- Exercise book
- Jumbo Crayon
- A stamp
- Object stamp
- Stamp pad

Presentation

- Bring out the required materials and place them on the table.
- Invite one child at a time to work with.
- Place the exercise book, crayon, and the stamp pad on the table for the child.
- Stamp the sound and the object on the exercise book.
- Ask the pupil to point at the objects
- Give the pupil the blue crayon to color the "r" sound.
- Give the pupil the yellow crayon to color the object.

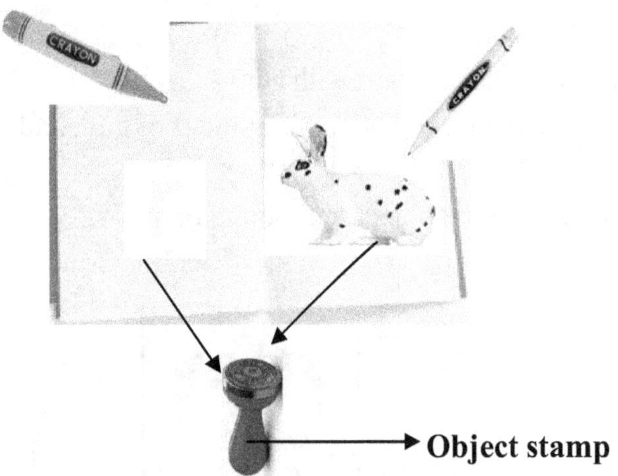

Colour the stamped sound "r" in the exercise book with blue crayon

Colour the stamped object rabbit in the exercise book with yellow crayon

Day 5

Pasting of Sound with Object "r" as in ruler.

Materials

- Creative reading worksheets
- Gum
- Cutout of sound with object "r" as in rat.

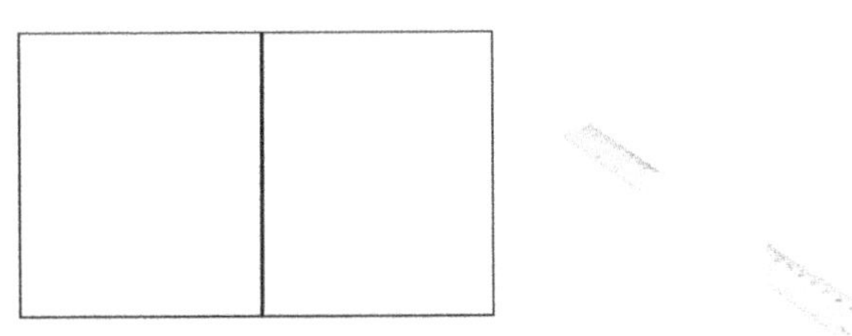

Presentation

- Bring out the required materials and place them on the table.
- Tell the pupils the name of the materials you have on the table.
- Call the pupils one by one to pick the cutout of sound with object "r" as in ruler.
- Demonstrate to them how to wet the sound pelican card with gum.
- Allow them all to wet the back of the sound with object cutout with considerable amount of gum.
- Bring out their worksheets and let them paste the object with sound on it.

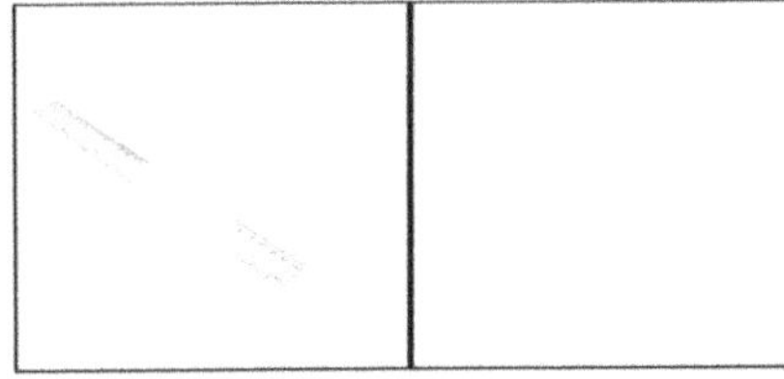

Paste the object with sound on the worksheet

WEEK 19: IDENTIFICATION OF SOUND "s"

Day 1

Reading of Sound "s"

Materials

- 3 Flash cards ("s" as sun, ship, star)
- Phonics bag.

Presentation

- Bring out the three flash cards.
- Place the cards on the table.
- Assemble the pupils together
- Read the sound and the object to the pupils and also ensure to show the body demonstration.
- Allow the pupils to pass the flash cards around.
- Return the flash cards to the phonics bag.
- Hang the bag back on the wall.

Day 2

Pasting of Sound "s" on Worksheet

Materials:

- My Phonics worksheet
- Pelican card of "s" sound
- Water gum
- Tray
- Towel

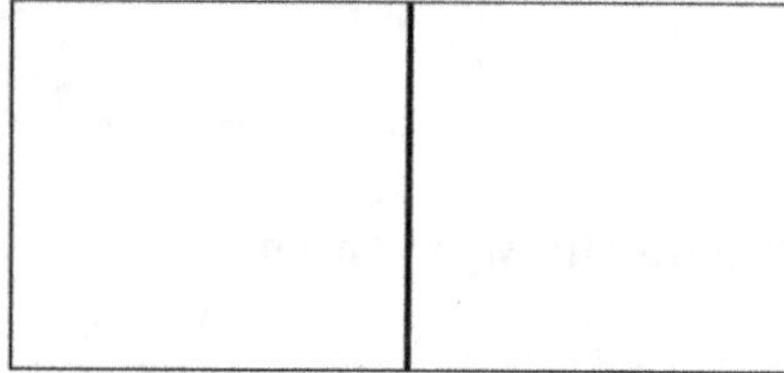

Presentation

- Bring out the required materials and place them on the table.
- Tell the pupils the name of the materials you have on the table.
- Call the pupils one by one to pick the "s" sound
- Provide them with a gum.
- Demonstrate to them how to wet the sound's pelican card with gum
- Allow them all to wet the back of the sound with considerable amount of gum.
- Provide each pupil with their own Jolly phonics worksheet.
- Allow the pupils to paste the sound "s" on the provided worksheet.

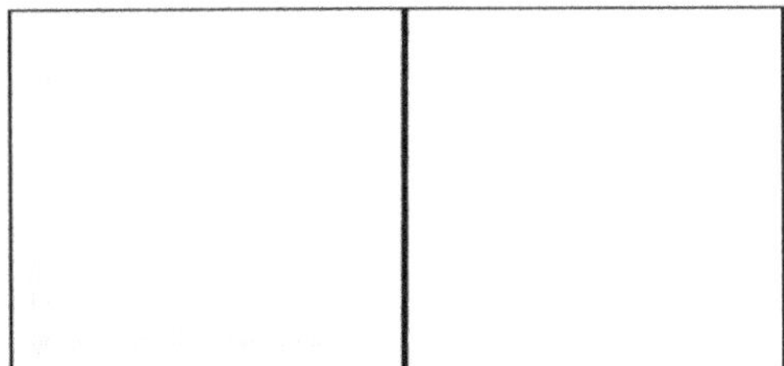

Paste the sound "s" Pelican card on the worksheet

Day 3

Pasting of Sound on Object

Materials

- Creative reading worksheets
- Gum
- Cutout object of ship
- cutout of sound "s"
- Tray

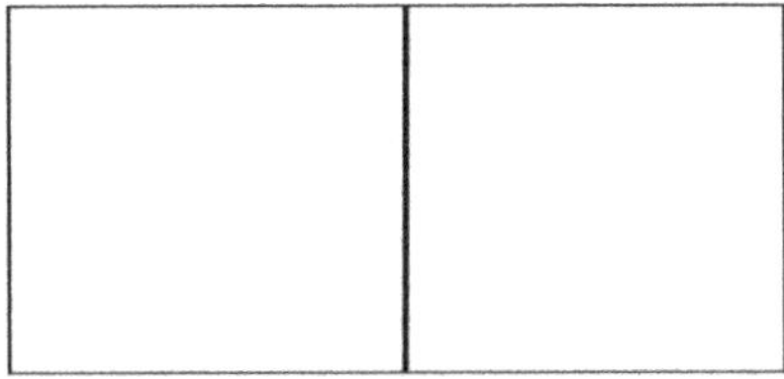 

- **Presentation**
- Bring out the required materials and place them on the table.
- Tell the pupils the name of the materials you have on the table.
- Call the pupils one by one to pick the "s" sound
- Demonstrate to them how to wet the sound pelican card with gum
- Allow them all to wet the back of the sound with considerable amount of gum and then paste it on the cutout object of ship.
- Bring out their worksheets and let them paste the object with sound on it.

Paste the cutout of sound "s" on the object ship

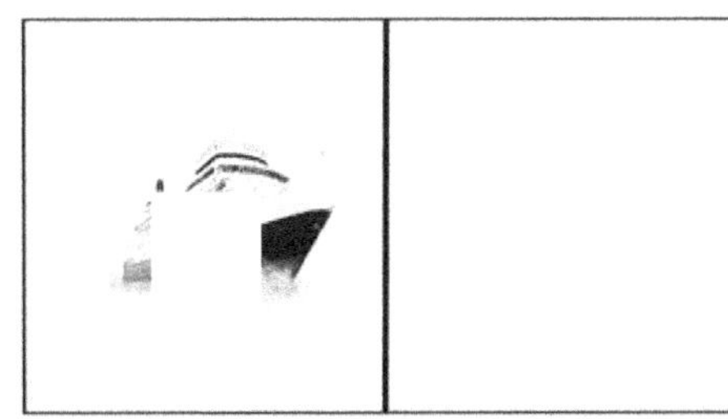

Paste the object ship with sound "s" on the worksheet

Day 4

Colouring of Sound with Object

Materials

- Exercise book
- Jumbo Crayon
- A stamp
- Object stamp
- Stamp pad

Presentation

- Bring out the required materials and place them on the table.
- Invite one child at a time to work with.
- Place the exercise book, crayon, and the stamp pad on the table for the child.
- Stamp the sound and the object on the exercise book.
- Ask the pupil to point at the objects
- Give the pupil the blue crayon to color the "s" sound.
- Give the pupil the yellow crayon to color the object.

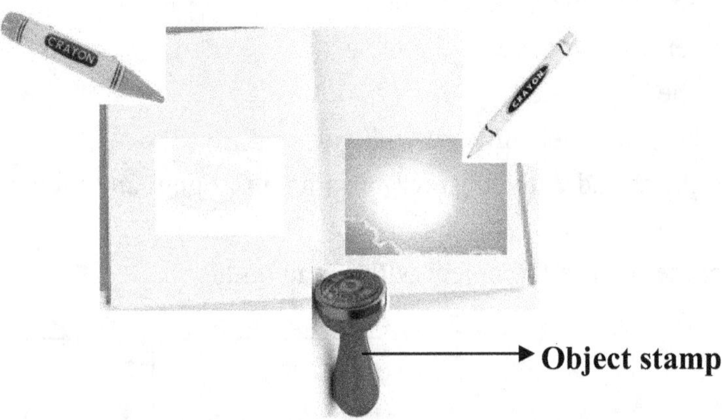

Colour the stamped sound "s" in the exercise book with blue crayon

Colour the stamped object sun in the exercise book with yellow crayon

Day 5

Pasting of Sound with Object "s" as star.

Materials

- Creative reading worksheets
- Gum
- Cutout of sound with object "s" as in star.

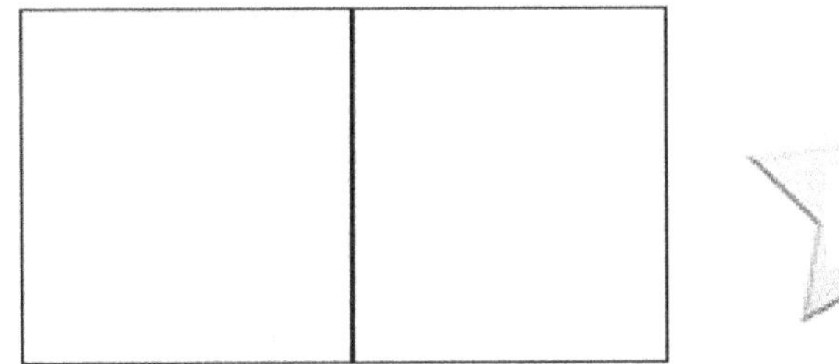

Presentation

- Bring out the required materials and place them on the table.
- Tell the pupils the name of the materials you have on the table.
- Call the pupils one by one to pick the cutout of sound with object "s" as in start.
- Demonstrate to them how to wet the sound's pelican card with gum.
- Allow them all to wet the back of the sound with object cutout with considerable amount of gum.
- Bring out their worksheets and let them paste the object with sound on it.

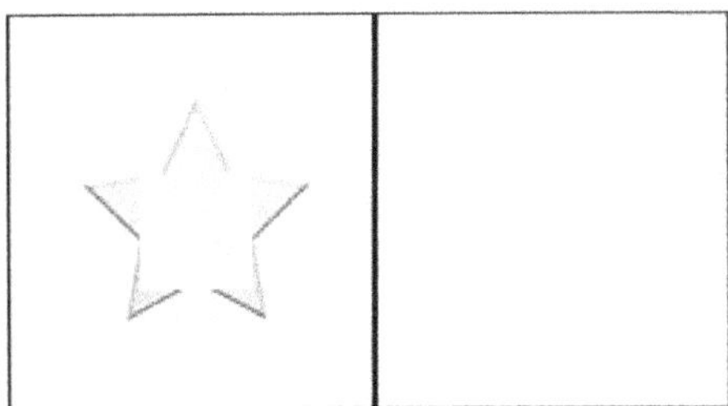

Paste the object with sound on the worksheet

WEEK 20: IDENTIFICATION OF SOUND "t"

Reading of Sound "t"

Materials

- 3 Flash cards ("t" as in toy, tap, tie)
- Phonics bag.

Presentation

- Bring out the three flash cards.
- Place the cards on the table.
- Assemble the pupils together
- Read the sound and the object to the pupils and also ensure to show the body demonstration.
- Allow the pupils to pass the flash cards around.
- Return the flash cards to the phonics bag.
- Hang the bag back on the wall.

Day 2

Pasting of Sound "t" on Worksheet

Materials:

- My Phonics worksheet
- Pelican card of "t" sound
- Water gum
- Tray
- Towel

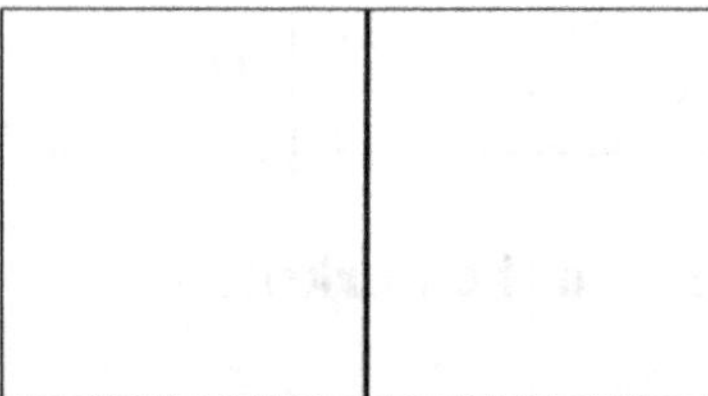

Presentation

- Bring out the required materials and place them on the table.
- Tell the pupils the name of the materials you have on the table.
- Call the pupils one by one to pick the "t" sound
- Provide them with a gum.
- Demonstrate to them how to wet the sound pelican card with gum
- Allow them all to wet the back of the sound with considerable amount of gum.
- Provide each pupil with their own Jolly phonics worksheet.
- Allow the pupils to paste the sound "t" on the provided worksheet.

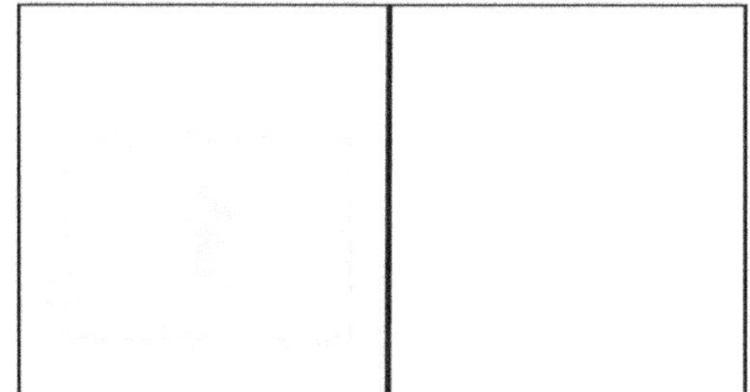

Paste the sound "t" Pelican card on the worksheet

Day 3

Pasting of Sound on Object

Materials

- Creative reading worksheets
- Gum
- Cutout object of ball
- cutout of sound "t"
- Tray

Presentation

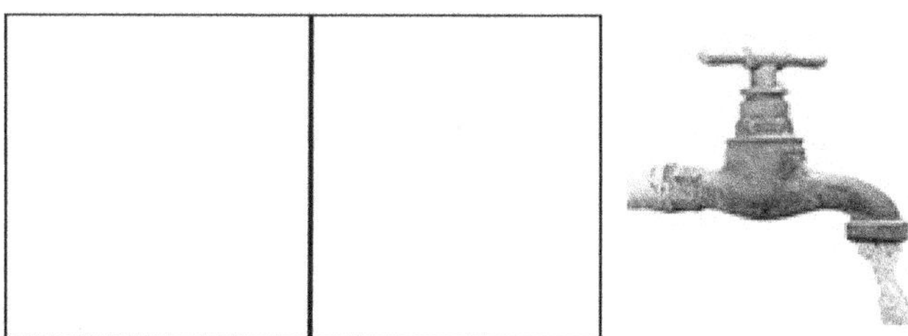

- Bring out the required materials and place them on the table.
- Tell the pupils the name of the materials you have on the table.
- Call the pupils one by one to pick the "t" sound
- Demonstrate to them how to wet the sound pelican card with gum
- Allow them all to wet the back of the sound with considerable amount of gum and then paste it on the cutout object of tap.
- Bring out their worksheets and let them paste the object with sound on it.

Paste the cutout of sound "t" on the object tap

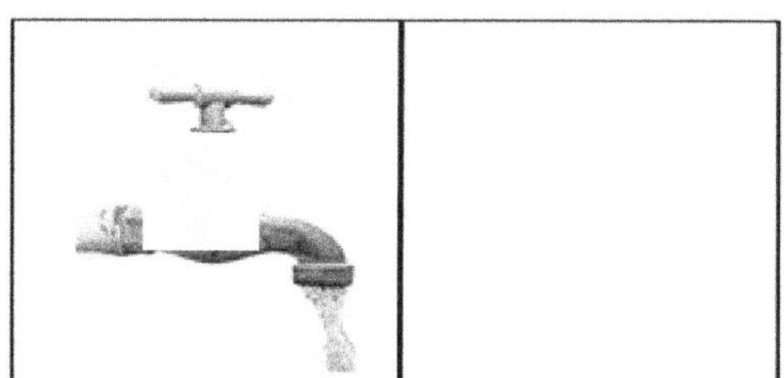

paste the object tap with sound "t" on the worksheet

Day 4

Colouring of Sound with Object

Materials

- Exercise book
- Jumbo Crayon

- A stamp
- Object stamp

- Stamp pad

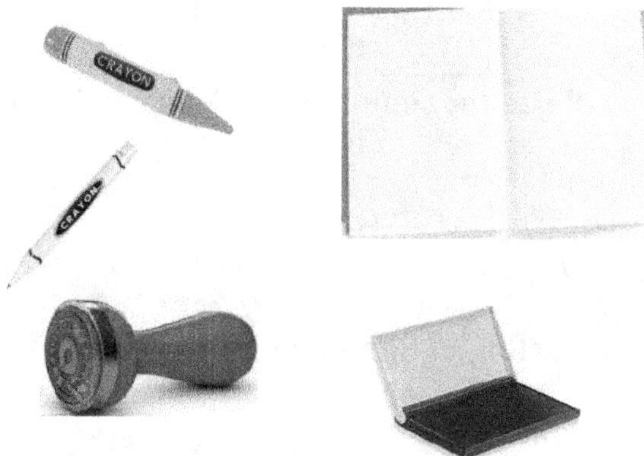

Presentation

- Bring out the required materials and place them on the table.
- Invite one child at a time to work with.
- Place the exercise book, crayon, and the stamp pad on the table for the child.
- Stamp the sound and the object on the exercise book.
- Ask the pupil to point at the objects
- Give the pupil the blue crayon to color the "t" sound.
- Give the pupil the yellow crayon to color the object.

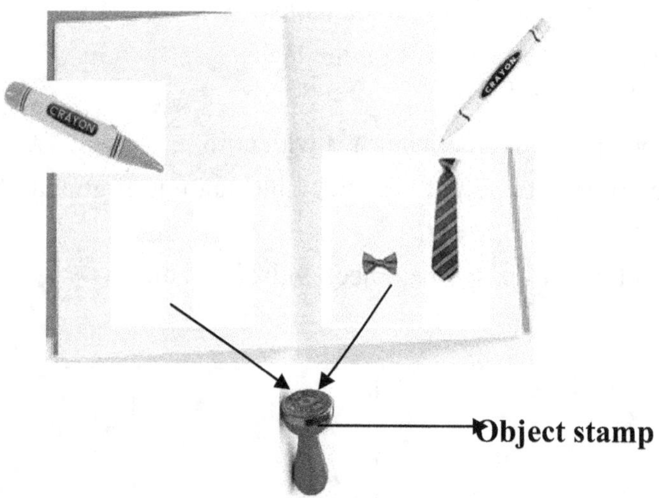

Colour the stamped sound "t" in the exercise book with blue crayon

Colour the stamped object tie in the exercise book with yellow crayon

Day 5

Pasting of Sound with Object "t" as toy

Materials

- Creative reading worksheets
- Gum
- Cutout of sound with object "t" as in train.

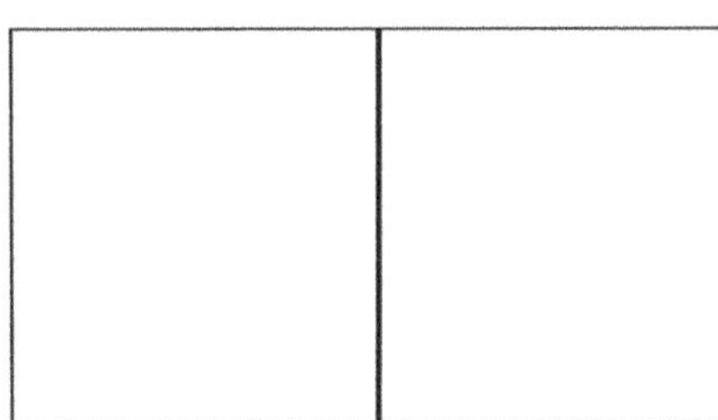 

Presentation

- Bring out the required materials and place them on the table.
- Tell the pupils the name of the materials you have on the table.
- Call the pupils one by one to pick the cutout of sound with object "t" as in toy.
- Demonstrate to them how to wet the sound pelican card with gum.
- Allow them all to wet the back of the sound with object cutout with considerable amount of gum.
- Bring out their worksheets and let them paste the object with sound on it.

Paste the object with sound on the worksheet

Reading of Sound "u"

Materials

- 3 Flash cards ("u" as umbrella, umpire, unicorn)
- Phonics bag.

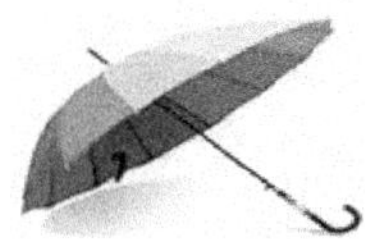

Presentation

- Bring out the three flash cards.
- Place the cards on the table.
- Assemble the pupils together
- Read the sound and the object to the pupils and also ensure to show the body demonstration.
- Allow the pupils to pass the flash cards around.
- Return the flash cards to the phonics bag.
- Hang the bag back on the wall.

Day 2

Pasting of Sound "u" on Worksheet

Materials:

- My Phonics worksheet
- Pelican card of "u" sound
- Water gum
- Tray
- Towel

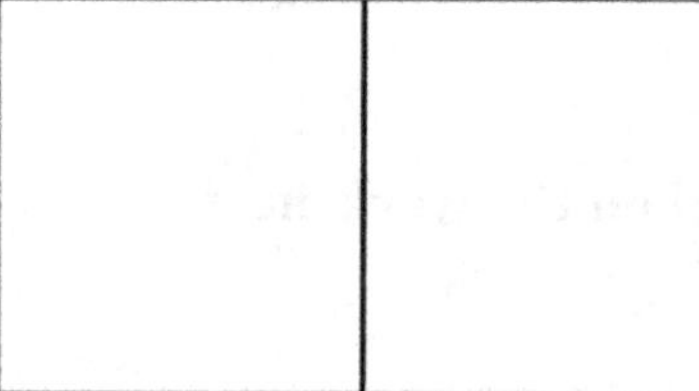

Presentation

- Bring out the required materials and place them on the table.
- Tell the pupils the name of the materials you have on the table.
- Call the pupils one by one to pick the "u" sound
- Provide them with a gum.
- Demonstrate to them how to wet the sound pelican card with gum
- Allow them all to wet the back of the sound with considerable amount of gum.
- Provide each pupil with their own Jolly phonics worksheet.

- Allow the pupils to paste the sound "u" on the provided worksheet.

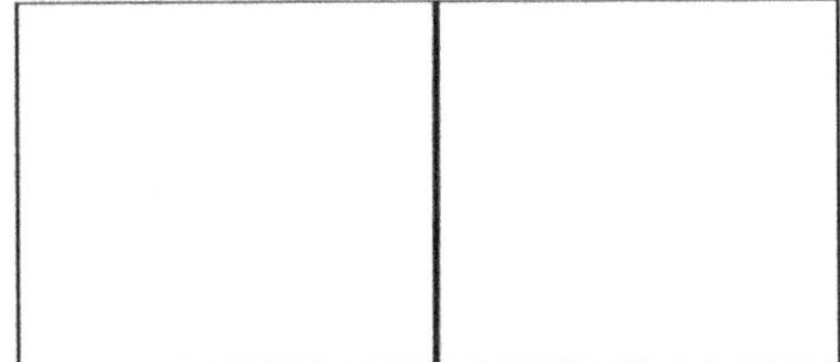

Paste the sound "u" Pelican card on the worksheet

Day 3

Pasting of Sound on Object

Materials

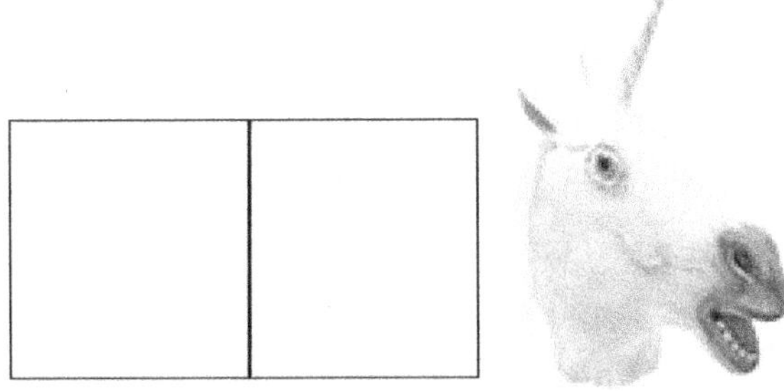

- Creative reading worksheets
- Gum
- Cutout object of ball
- cutout of sound "u"
- Tray

- **Presentation**
- Bring out the required materials and place them on the table.
- Tell the pupils the name of the materials you have on the table.
- Call the pupils one by one to pick the "t" sound
- Demonstrate to them how to wet the sound pelican card with gum
- Allow them all to wet the back of the sound with considerable amount of gum and then paste it on the cutout object of unicorn.
- Bring out their worksheets and let them paste the object with sound on it.

Paste the cutout of sound "u" on the object unicorn

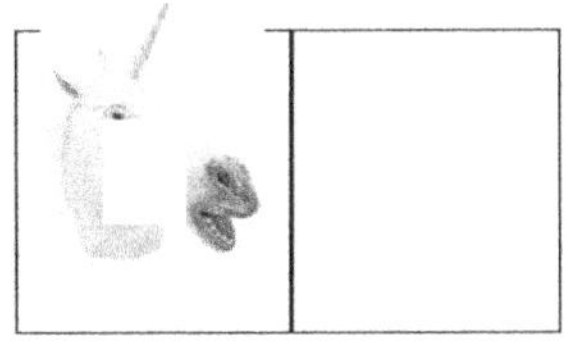

Paste the object unicorn with sound "u" on the worksheet

Day 4

Colouring of Sound with Object

Materials

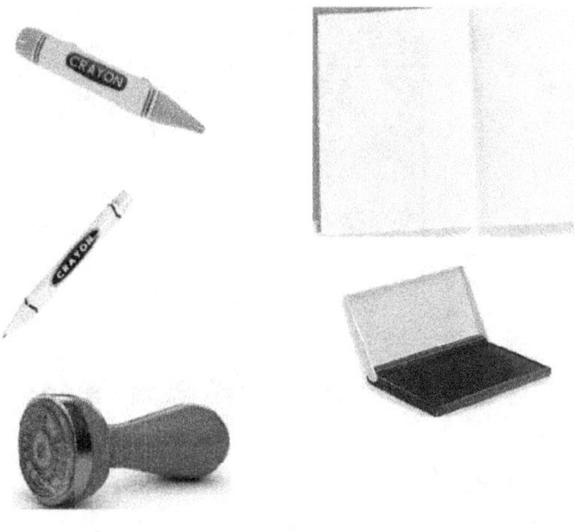

- Exercise book
- Jumbo Crayon
- A stamp
- Object stamp
- Stamp pad

Presentation

- Bring out the required materials and place them on the table.
- Invite one child at a time to work with.
- Place the exercise book, crayon, and the stamp pad on the table for the child.
- Stamp the sound and the object on the exercise book.
- Ask the pupil to point at the objects
- Give the pupil the blue crayon to color the "u" sound.
- Give the pupil the yellow crayon to color the object.

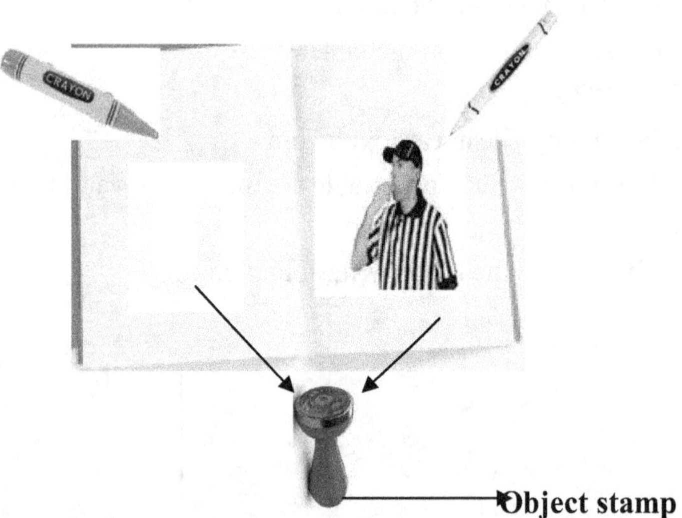

Colour the stamped sound "u" in the exercise book with blue crayon

Colour the stamped object umpire in the exercise book with yellow crayon

Day 5

Pasting of Sound with Object "u" as in umbrella.

Materials

- Creative reading worksheets
- Gum
- Cutout of sound with object "u" as in umbrella.

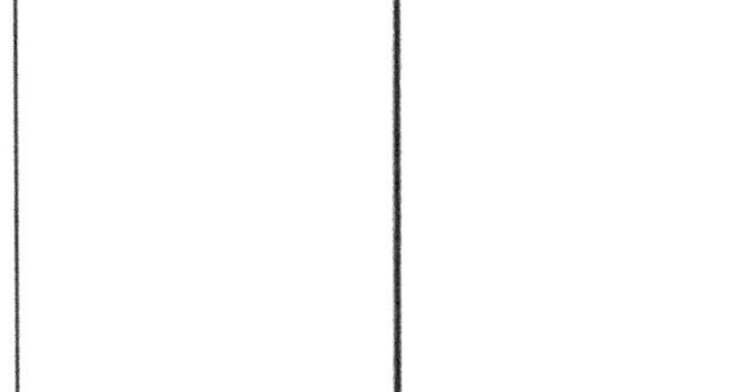 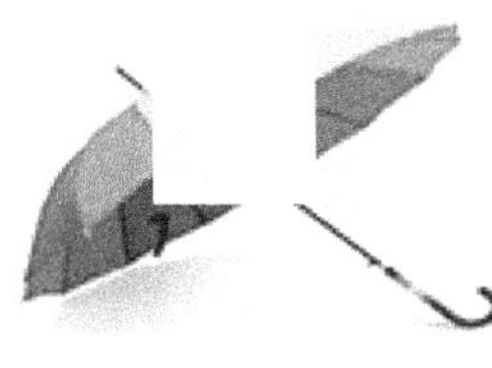

Presentation

- Bring out the required materials and place them on the table.
- Tell the pupils the name of the materials you have on the table.
- Call the pupils one by one to pick the cutout of sound with object "u" as in umbrella.
- Demonstrate to them how to wet the sound pelican card with gum.
- Allow them all to wet the back of the sound with object cutout with considerable amount of gum.
- Bring out their worksheets and let them paste the object with sound on it.

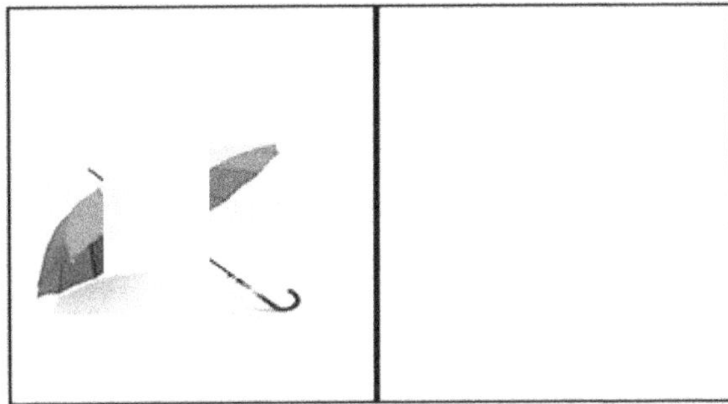

Paste the object with sound on the worksheet

Reading of Sound "v"

Materials

- 3 Flash cards ("v" as in vest, violin, van)
- Phonics bag.

Presentation

- Bring out the three flash cards.
- Place the cards on the table.
- Assemble the pupils together
- Read the sound and the object to the pupils and also ensure to show the body demonstration.
- Allow the pupils to pass the flash cards around.
- Return the flash cards to the phonics bag.
- Hang the bag back on the wall.

Day 2

Pasting of Sound "v" on Worksheet

Materials:

- My Phonics worksheet
- Pelican card of "v" sound
- Water gum
- Tray
- Towel

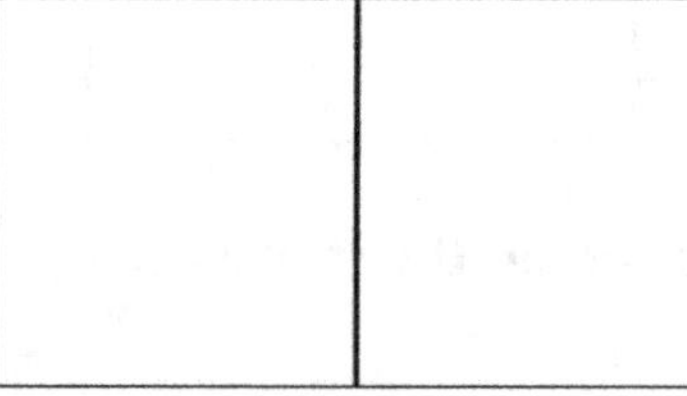

Presentation

- Bring out the required materials and place them on the table.
- Tell the pupils the name of the materials you have on the table.
- Call the pupils one by one to pick the "u" sound
- Provide them with a gum.
- Demonstrate to them how to wet the sound pelican card with gum
- Allow them all to wet the back of the sound with considerable amount of gum.
- Provide each pupil with their own Jolly phonics worksheet.
- Allow the pupils to paste the sound "u" on the provided worksheet.

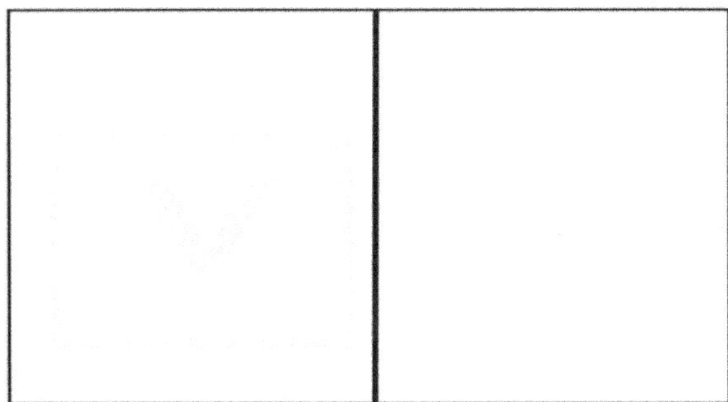

Paste the sound "v" Pelican card on the worksheet

Day 3

Pasting of Sound on Object

Materials

- Creative reading worksheets
- Gum
- Cutout object of ball
- cutout of sound "v"
- Tray

Presentation

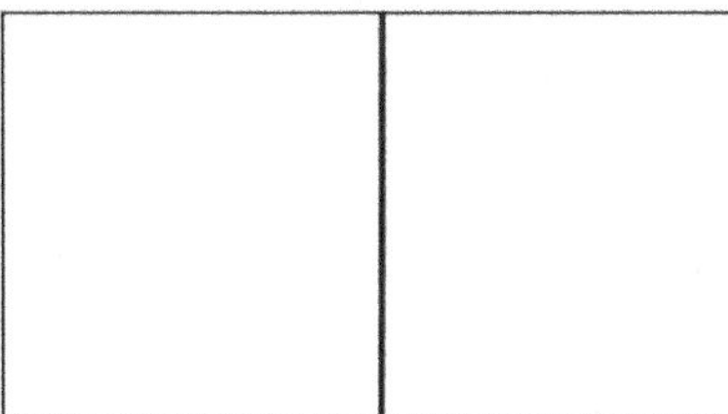

- Bring out the required materials and place them on the table.
- Tell the pupils the name of the materials you have on the table.
- Call the pupils one by one to pick the "v" sound
- Demonstrate to them how to wet the sound pelican card with gum
- Allow them all to wet the back of the sound with considerable amount of gum and then paste it on the cutout object of van
- Bring out their worksheets and let them paste the object with sound on it.

Paste the cutout of sound "v" on the v van

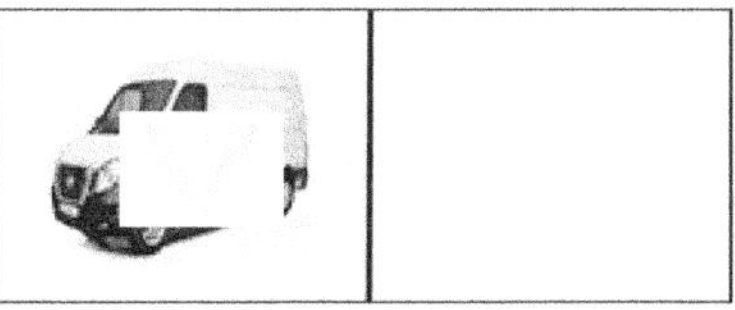

Paste the object van with sound "v" on the worksheet

Day 4

Colouring of Sound with Object

Materials

- Exercise book
- Jumbo Crayon
- A stamp
- Object stamp
- Stamp pad

Presentation

- Bring out the required materials and place them on the table.
- Invite one child at a time to work with.
- Place the exercise book, crayon, and the stamp pad on the table for the child.
- Stamp the sound and the object on the exercise book.
- Ask the pupil to point at the objects
- Give the pupil the blue crayon to color the "v" sound.
- Give the pupil the yellow crayon to color the object.

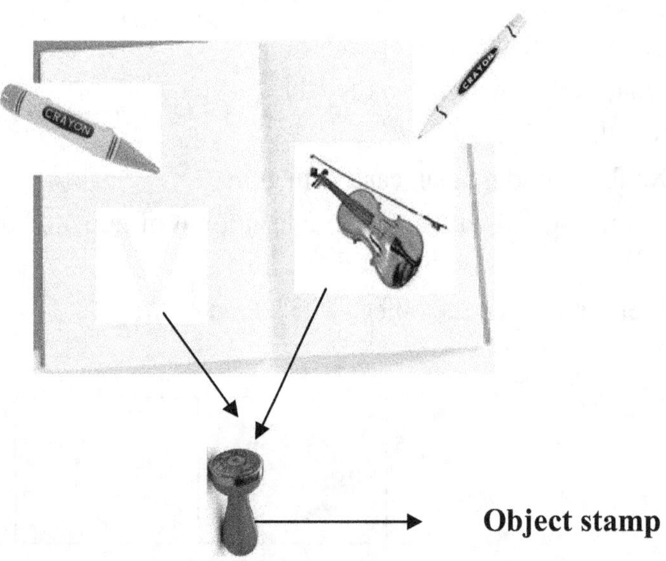

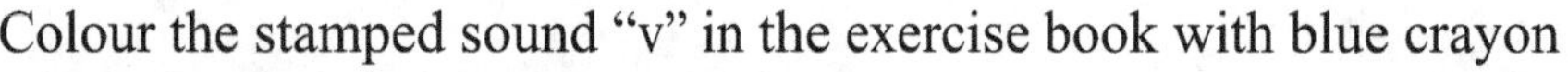

Colour the stamped sound "v" in the exercise book with blue crayon

Colour the stamped object violin in the exercise book with yellow crayon

Day 5

Pasting of Sound with Object "v" as in vest.

Materials

- Creative reading worksheets
- Gum
- Cutout of sound with object "v" as in vest.

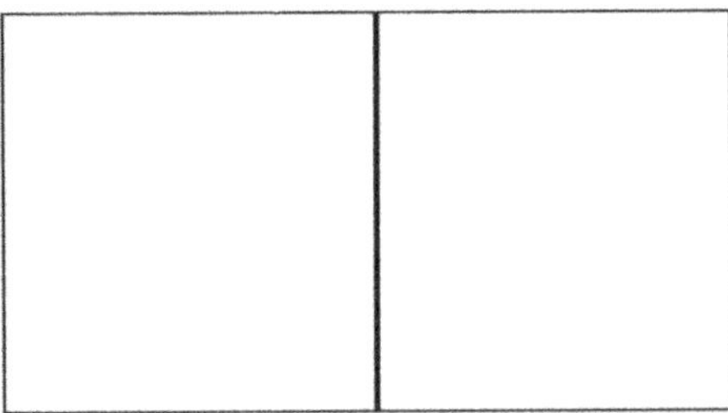

Presentation

- Bring out the required materials and place them on the table.
- Tell the pupils the name of the materials you have on the table.
- Call the pupils one by one to pick the cutout of sound with object "v" as in vest.
- Demonstrate to them how to wet the sound pelican card with gum.
- Allow them all to wet the back of the sound with object cutout with considerable amount of gum.
- Bring out their worksheets and let them paste the object with sound on it.

Paste the object with sound on the worksheet

<h1 style="text-align:center">WEEK 23: IDENTIFICATION OF SOUND "w"</h1>

Reading of Sound "w"

Materials

- 3 Flash cards ("w" as whale, window, watch)
- Phonics bag.
-

Presentation

- Bring out the three flash cards.
- Place the cards on the table.
- Assemble the pupils together
- Read the sound and the object to the pupils and also ensure to show the body demonstration.
- Allow the pupils to pass the flash cards around.
- Return the flash cards to the phonics bag.
- Hang the bag back on the wall.

Day 2

Pasting of Sound "w" on Worksheet

Materials:

- My Phonics worksheet
- Pelican card of "w" sound
- Water gum
- Tray
- Towel

Presentation

- Bring out the required materials and place them on the table.
- Tell the pupils the name of the materials you have on the table.
- Call the pupils one by one to pick the "w" sound
- Provide them with a gum.
- Demonstrate to them how to wet the sound pelican card with gum
- Allow them all to wet the back of the sound with considerable amount of gum.
- Provide each pupil with their own Jolly phonics worksheet.
- Allow the pupils to paste the sound "w" on the provided worksheet.

96

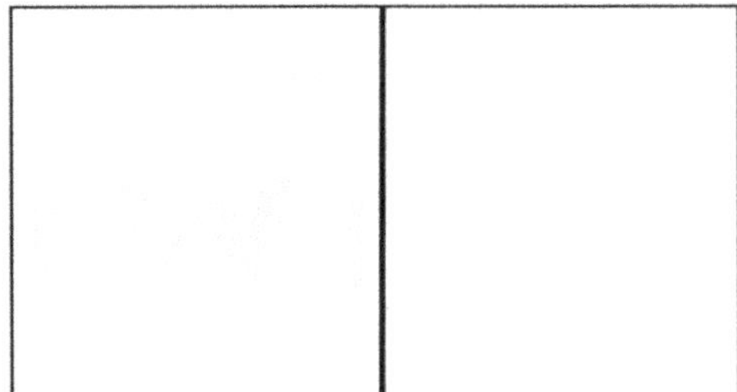

Paste the sound "w" Pelican card on the worksheet

Day 3

Pasting of Sound on Object

Materials

- Creative reading worksheets
- Gum
- Cutout object of ball
- cutout of sound "w"
- Tray

Presentation

- Bring out the required materials and place them on the table.
- Tell the pupils the name of the materials you have on the table.
- Call the pupils one by one to pick the "w" sound
- Demonstrate to them how to wet the sound pelican card with gum
- Allow them all to wet the back of the sound with considerable amount of gum and then paste it on the cutout object of window.
- Bring out their worksheets and let them paste the object with sound on it.

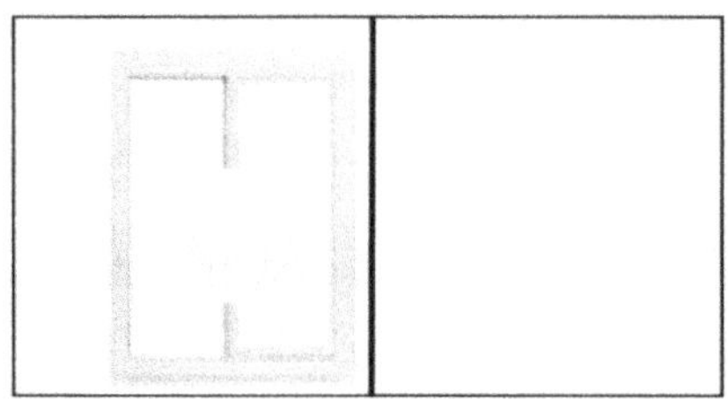

Paste the cutout of sound "w" on the object window

Paste the object window with sound "w" on the worksheet

Day 4

Colouring of Sound with Object

Materials

- Exercise book
- Jumbo Crayon
- A stamp
- Object stamp
- Stamp pad

Presentation

- Bring out the required materials and place them on the table.
- Invite one child at a time to work with.
- Place the exercise book, crayon, and the stamp pad on the table for the child.
- Stamp the sound and the object on the exercise book.
- Ask the pupil to point at the objects
- Give the pupil the blue crayon to color the "w" sound.
- Give the pupil the yellow crayon to color the object.

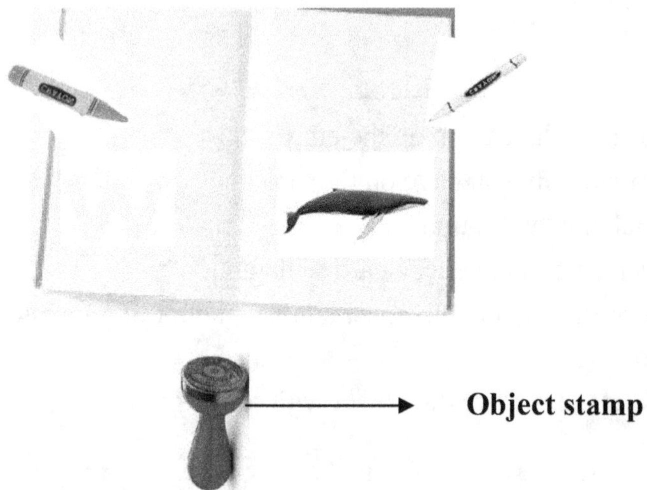

Colour the stamped sound "w" in the exercise book with blue crayon

Colour the stamped object whale in the exercise book with yellow crayon

Day 5

Pasting of Sound with Object "w" as in watch.

Materials

- Creative reading worksheets
- Gum
- Cutout of sound with object "w" as in watch.

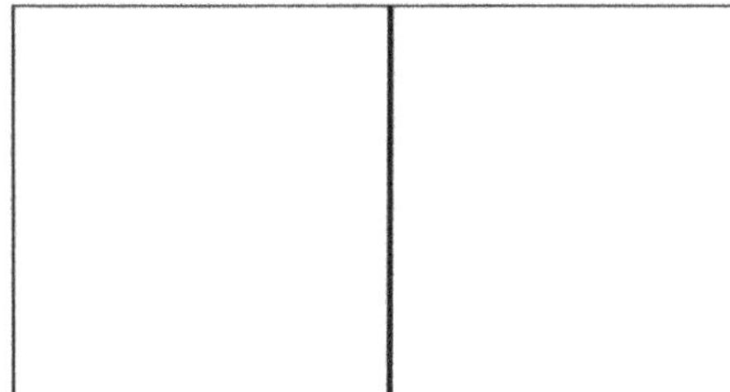 

Presentation

- Bring out the required materials and place them on the table.
- Tell the pupils the name of the materials you have on the table.
- Call the pupils one by one to pick the cutout of sound with object "w" as in vest.
- Demonstrate to them how to wet the sound pelican card with gum.
- Allow them all to wet the back of the sound with object cutout with considerable amount of gum.
- Bring out their worksheets and let them paste the object with sound on it.

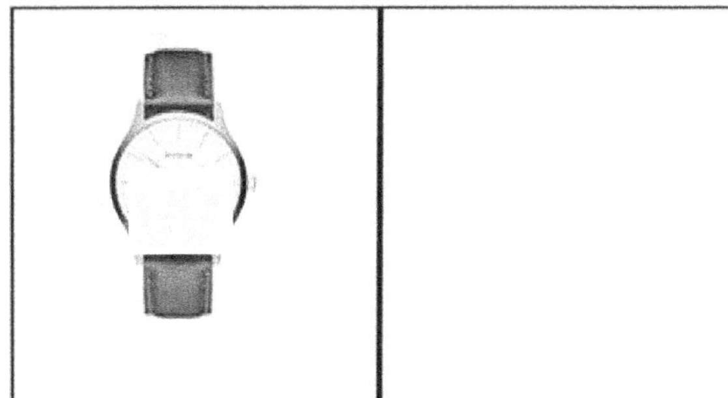

Paste the object with sound on the worksheet

WEEK 24: IDENTIFICATION OF SOUND "x"

Reading of Sound "x"

Materials

- 3 Flash cards ("x" as xylophone, x-ray, xmas tree)
- Phonics bag.

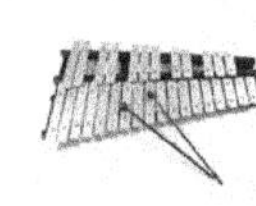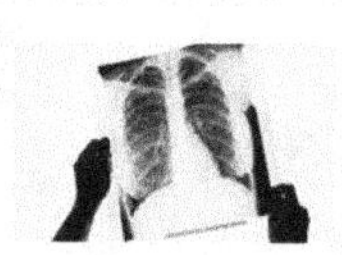

Presentation

- Bring out the three flash cards.
- Place the cards on the table.
- Assemble the pupils together
- Read the sound and the object to the pupils and also ensure to show the body demonstration.
- Allow the pupils to pass the flash cards around.
- Return the flash cards to the phonics bag.
- Hang the bag back on the wall.

Day 2

Pasting of Sound "x" on Worksheet

Materials:

- My Phonics worksheet
- Pelican card of "x" sound
- Water gum
- Tray
- Towel

Presentation

- Bring out the required materials and place them on the table.
- Tell the pupils the name of the materials you have on the table.
- Call the pupils one by one to pick the "x" sound
- Provide them with a gum.
- Demonstrate to them how to wet the sound pelican card with gum
- Allow them all to wet the back of the sound with considerable amount of gum.
- Provide each pupil with their own Jolly phonics worksheet.
- Allow the pupils to paste the sound "x" on the provided worksheet.

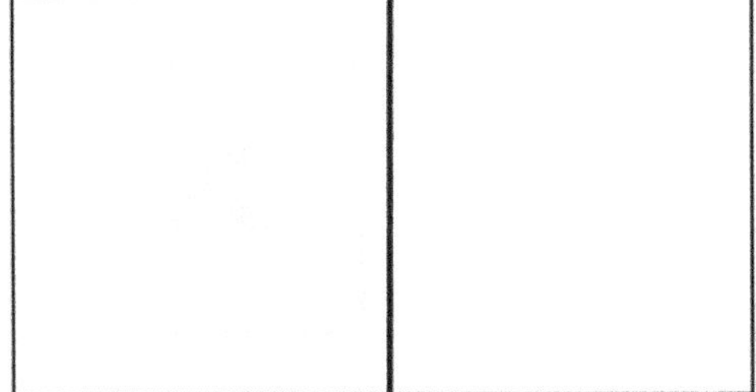

Paste the sound "x" Pelican card on the worksheet

Day 3

Pasting of Sound on Object

Materials

- Creative reading worksheets
- Gum
- Cutout object of xylophone
- cutout of sound "x"
- Tray

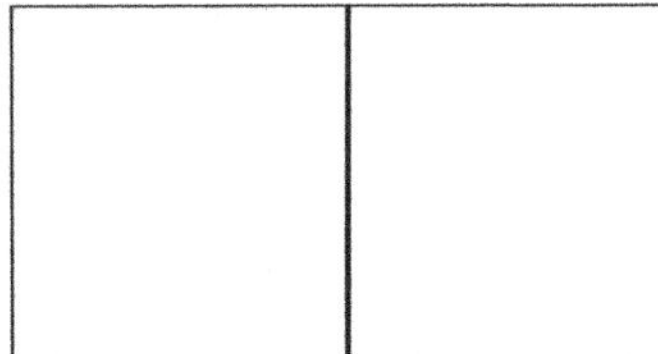

Presentation

- Bring out the required materials and place them on the table.
- Tell the pupils the name of the materials you have on the table.
- Call the pupils one by one to pick the "x" sound
- Demonstrate to them how to wet the sound pelican card with gum
- Allow them all to wet the back of the sound with considerable amount of gum and then paste it on the cutout object of xylophone.
- Bring out their worksheets and let them paste the object with sound on it.

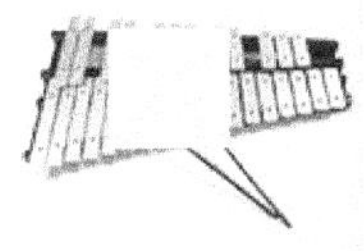

Paste the cutout of sound "x" on the object xylophone

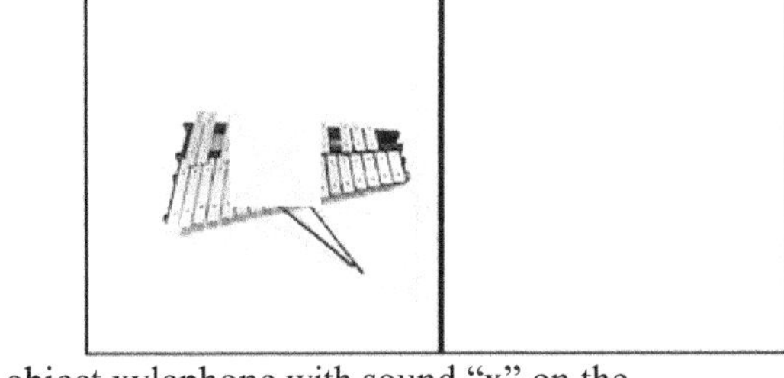

Paste the object xylophone with sound "x" on the worksheet

Day 4

Colouring of Sound with Object

Materials

- Exercise book
- Jumbo Crayon
- A stamp
- Object stamp
- Stamp pad

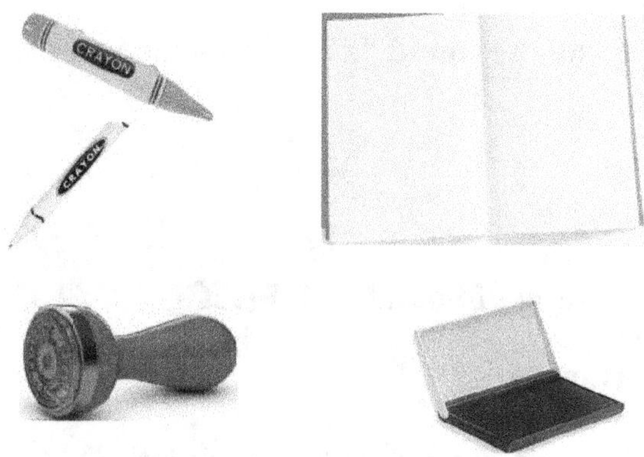

Presentation

- Bring out the required materials and place them on the table.
- Invite one child at a time to work with.
- Place the exercise book, crayon, and the stamp pad on the table for the child.
- Stamp the sound and the object on the exercise book.
- Ask the pupil to point at the objects
- Give the pupil the blue crayon to color the "x" sound.
- Give the pupil the yellow crayon to color the object.

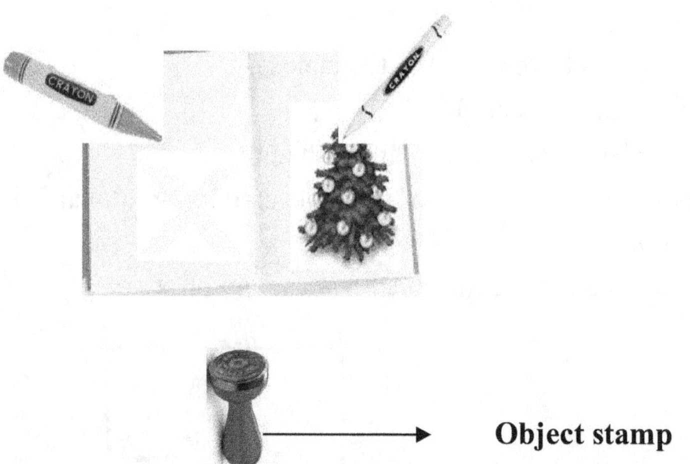

Object stamp

Colour the stamped sound "x" in the exercise book with blue crayon

Colour the stamped object xmas tree in the exercise book with yellow crayon

Day 5

Pasting of Sound with Object "x" as in xmas tree.

Materials

- Creative reading worksheets
- Gum
- Cutout of sound with object "x" as in xylophone.

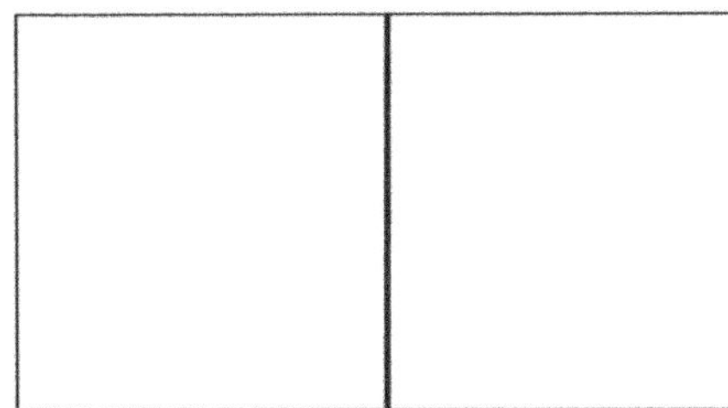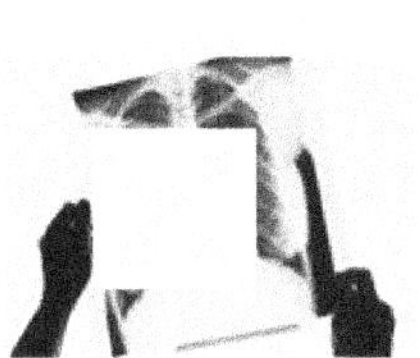

Presentation

- Bring out the required materials and place them on the table.
- Tell the pupils the name of the materials you have on the table.
- Call the pupils one by one to pick the cutout of sound with object "x" as in xylophone.
- Demonstrate to them how to wet the sound pelican card with gum.
- Allow them all to wet the back of the sound with object cutout with considerable amount of gum.
- Bring out their worksheets and let them paste the object with sound on it.

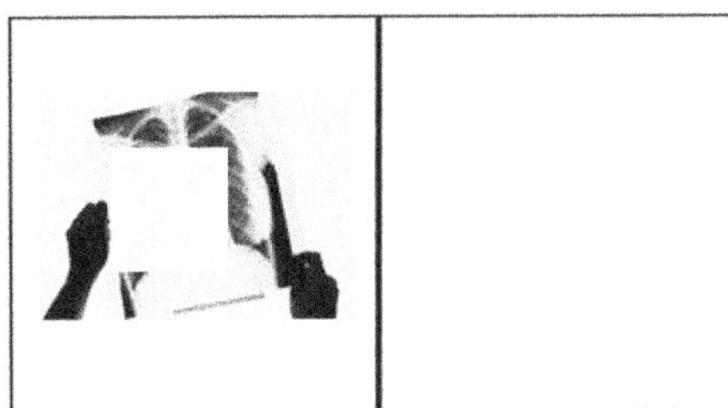

Paste the object with sound on the worksheet

Reading of Sound "y"

Materials

- 3 Flash cards ("y" as yam, yacht, yoyo)
- Phonics bag.

Presentation

- Bring out the three flash cards.
- Place the cards on the table.
- Assemble the pupils together
- Read the sound and the object to the pupils and also ensure to show the body demonstration.
- Allow the pupils to pass the flash cards around.
- Return the flash cards to the phonics bag.
- Hang the bag back on the wall.

Day 2

Pasting of Sound "y" on Worksheet

Materials:

- My Phonics worksheet
- Pelican card of "y" sound
- Water gum
- Tray
- Towel

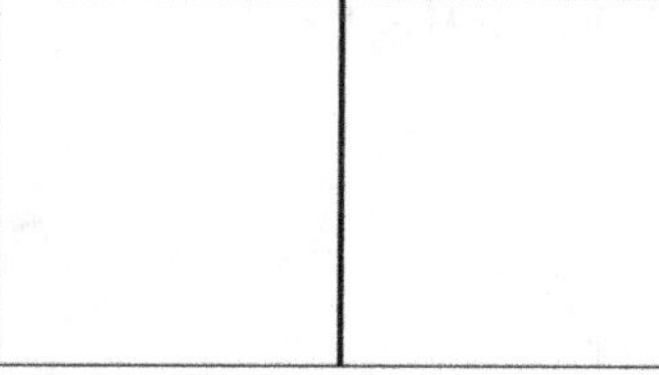

Presentation

- Bring out the required materials and place them on the table.
- Tell the pupils the name of the materials you have on the table.
- Call the pupils one by one to pick the "y" sound
- Provide them with a gum.
- Demonstrate to them how to wet the sound pelican card with gum
- Allow them all to wet the back of the sound with considerable amount of gum.
- Provide each pupil with their own Jolly phonics worksheet.
- Allow the pupils to paste the sound "y" on the provided worksheet.

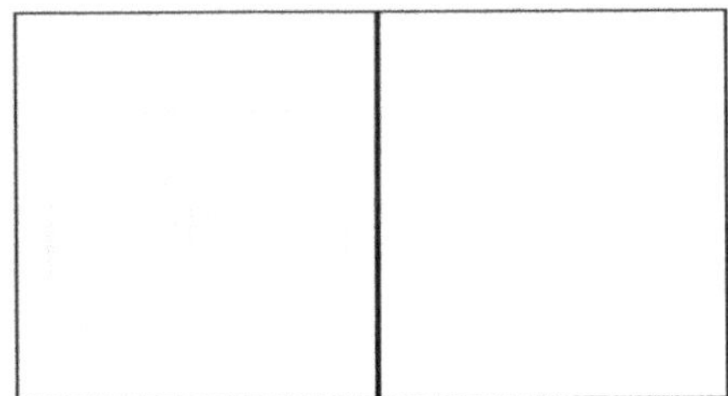

Paste the sound "y" Pelican card on the worksheet

Day 3

Pasting of Sound on Object

Materials

- Creative reading worksheets
- Gum
- Cutout object of yam
- cutout of sound "y"
- Tray

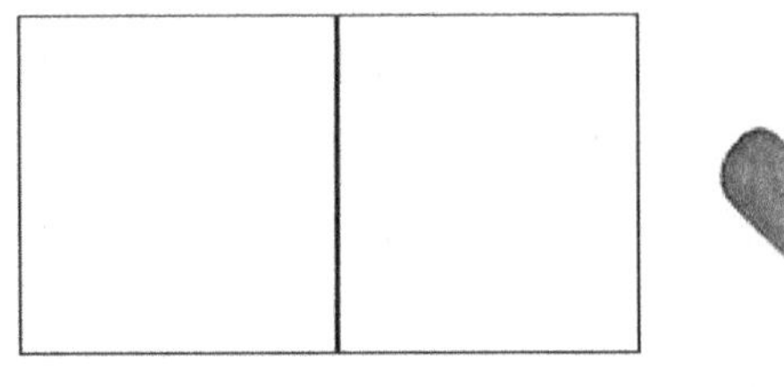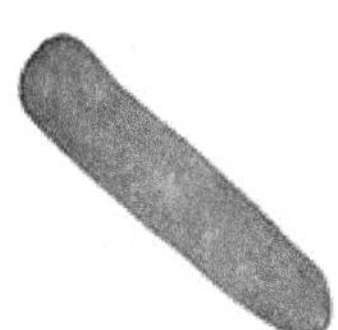

Presentation

- Bring out the required materials and place them on the table.
- Tell the pupils the name of the materials you have on the table.
- Call the pupils one by one to pick the "y" sound
- Demonstrate to them how to wet the sound pelican card with gum
- Allow them all to wet the back of the sound with considerable amount of gum and then paste it on the cutout object of yam.
- Bring out their worksheets and let them paste the object with sound on it.

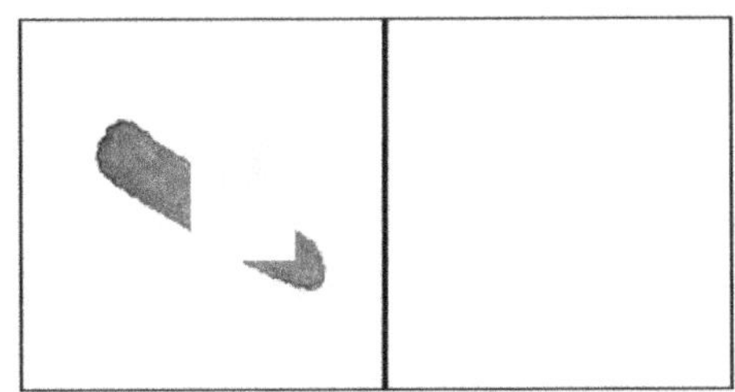

Paste the cutout of sound "y" on the object yam

Paste the object yam with sound "y" on the worksheet

Day 4

Colouring of Sound with Object

Materials

- Exercise book
- Jumbo Crayon
- A stamp
- Object stamp
- Stamp pad

Presentation

- Bring out the required materials and place them on the table.
- Invite one child at a time to work with.
- Place the exercise book, crayon, and the stamp pad on the table for the child.
- Stamp the sound and the object on the exercise book.
- Ask the pupil to point at the objects
- Give the pupil the blue crayon to color the "y" sound.
- Give the pupil the yellow crayon to color the object.

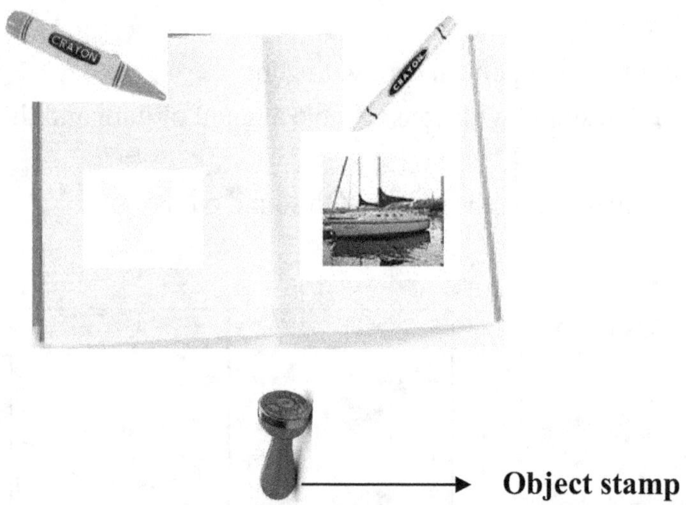

Colour the stamped sound "y" in the exercise book with blue crayon

Colour the stamped object yacht in the exercise book with yellow crayon

Day 5

Pasting of Sound with Object "y" as in yoyo

Materials

- Creative reading worksheets
- Gum
- Cutout of sound with object "y" as in yoyo

Presentation

- Bring out the required materials and place them on the table.
- Tell the pupils the name of the materials you have on the table.
- Call the pupils one by one to pick the cutout of sound with object "y" as in yoyo
- Demonstrate to them how to wet the sound pelican card with gum.
- Allow them all to wet the back of the sound with object cutout with considerable amount of gum.
- Bring out their worksheets and let them paste the object with sound on it.

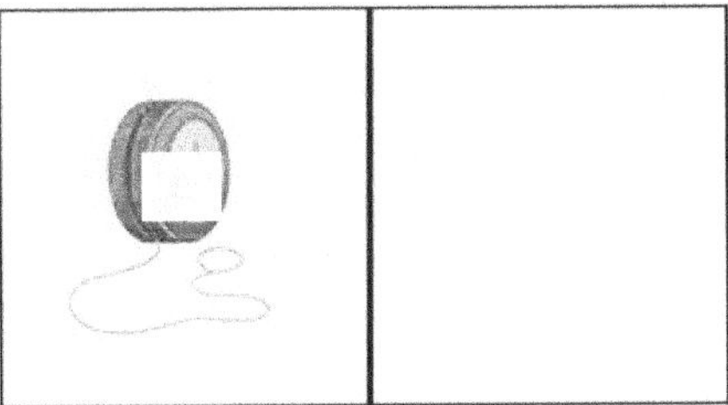

Paste the object with sound on the worksheet

Day1

Reading of Sound "z"

Materials

- 3 Flash cards ("z" as zebra, zipper, zero)
- Phonics bag.

Presentation

- Bring out the three flash cards.
- Place the cards on the table.
- Assemble the pupils together
- Read the sound and the object to the pupils and also ensure to show the body demonstration.
- Allow the pupils to pass the flash cards around.
- Return the flash cards to the phonics bag.
- Hang the bag back on the wall.

Day 2

Pasting of Sound "z" on Worksheet

Materials:

- My Phonics worksheet
- Pelican card of "z" sound
- Water gum
- Tray
- Towel

- **Presentation**
- Bring out the required materials and place them on the table.
- Tell the pupils the name of the materials you have on the table.
- Call the pupils one by one to pick the "z" sound
- Provide them with a gum.
- Demonstrate to them how to wet the sound pelican card with gum
- Allow them all to wet the back of the sound with considerable amount of gum.
- Provide each pupil with their own Jolly phonics worksheet.
- Allow the pupils to paste the sound "z" on the provided worksheet.

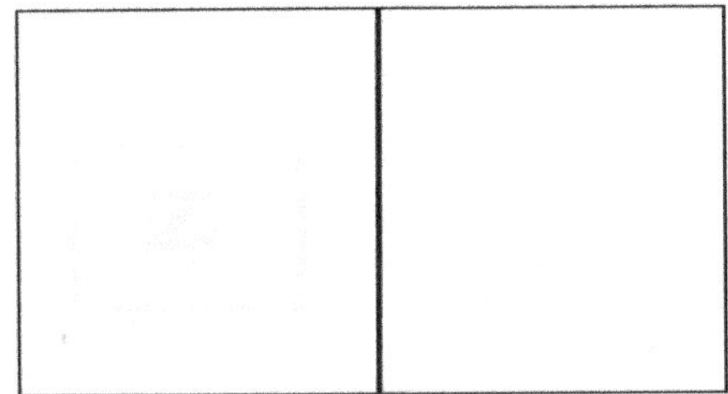

Paste the sound "z" Pelican card on the worksheet

Day 3

Pasting of Sound on Object

Materials

- Creative reading worksheets
- Gum
- Cutout object of ball
- cutout of sound "z"
- Tray

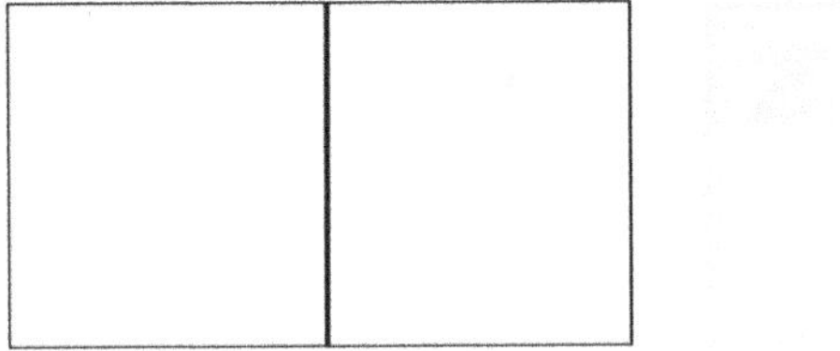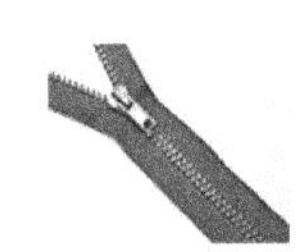

Presentation

- Bring out the required materials and place them on the table.
- Tell the pupils the name of the materials you have on the table.
- Call the pupils one by one to pick the "z" sound
- Demonstrate to them how to wet the sound pelican card with gum
- Allow them all to wet the back of the sound with considerable amount of gum and then paste it on the cutout object of zipper.
- Bring out their worksheets and let them paste the object with sound on it.

Paste the cutout of sound "z" on the object zipper

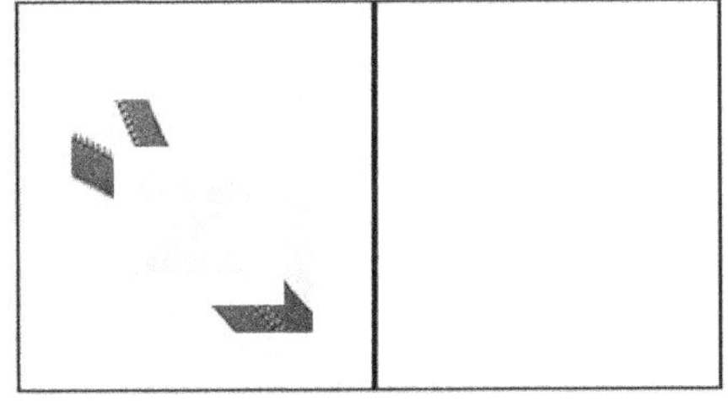

Paste the object zipper with sound "z" on the worksheet

Day 4

Colouring of Sound with Object

Materials

- Exercise book
- Jumbo Crayon
- A stamp
- Object stamp
- Stamp pad

Presentation

- Bring out the required materials and place them on the table.
- Invite one child at a time to work with.
- Place the exercise book, crayon, and the stamp pad on the table for the child.
- Stamp the sound and the object on the exercise book.
- Ask the pupil to point at the objects
- Give the pupil the blue crayon to color the "z" sound.
- Give the pupil the yellow crayon to color the object.

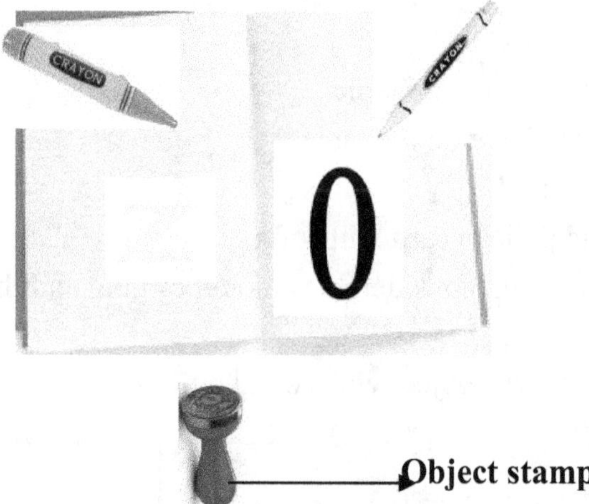

Colour the stamped sound "z" in the exercise book with blue crayon

Colour the stamped object zero in the exercise book with yellow crayon

Day 5

Pasting of Sound with Object "z" as in zebra.

Materials

- Creative reading worksheets
- Gum
- Cutout of sound with object "z" as in zebra.

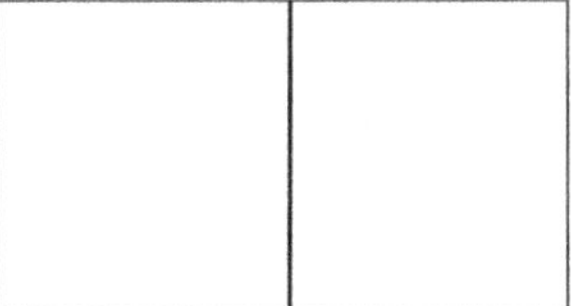

Presentation

- Bring out the required materials and place them on the table.
- Tell the pupils the name of the materials you have on the table.
- Call the pupils one by one to pick the cutout of sound with object "z" as in zebra.
- Demonstrate to them how to wet the sound's pelican card with gum.
- Allow them all to wet the back of the sound with object cutout with considerable amount of gum.
- Bring out their worksheets and let them paste the object with sound on it.

Paste the object with sound on the worksheet

REFRENCES

British Children Curriculum

Montessori Primary Guide (infomontessori.com)

Early Years Foundation Curriculum

Google images

www.ingramcontent.com/pod-product-compliance
Lightning Source LLC
Chambersburg PA
CBHW081308250726
48662CB00008B/2453